Preaching

God's Burning Word

by

James M. Reese, O.S.F.S.

THE LITURGICAL PRESS

Collegeville, Minnesota

Cover photo from Discovery Series, *courtesy* Paulist Press.

Imprimi potest: Daniel G. Gambet, O.S.F.S., *Provincial. Nihil obstat:* William Heidt, O.S.B., *Censor deputatus. Imprimatur:* ✝ George H. Speltz, D.D., Bishop of St. Cloud, St. Cloud, Minnesota, July 18, 1975.

ISBN 0-8146-0886-8.

TABLE OF CONTENTS

Preface

These chapters are the fruit of my efforts to foster biblical preaching as an associate of the Word of God Institute. Participation in courses and workshops on biblical preaching has deepened my conviction of the importance that preaching is destined to play in the life of the Christian community. Preachers and other religious educators must proclaim the conviction of the important role they play in God's reconciling love. But conviction is not simply enough.

Obviously, preachers must know the Scripture they handle. And they must know more than Scripture. The strong emphasis in these chapters on literary competence expresses my conviction that good preaching demands knowledge of how language works.

In these talks will be found the theory that underlies the Burning Word series found in *The* BIBLE *Today*. That series of pastoral preaching articles rests upon the principles, ideals and goals discussed in this work. Only by prayerful reflection and ongoing practice will biblical preaching and other forms of religious persuasion build up the Church.

My thanks to Fr. John Burke, O.P., executive director, and to William Graham, associate director of the Word of God Institute for the privilege of sharing in the preaching apostolate. Special thanks to Sister Eileen Storey, S.C., for her editorial aid in preparing these manuscripts for publication.

1.

The Burning Word as Prophetic Voice

To nourish the faith-life that God communicates to believers as a gift: this is the essential purpose of homilies. The chapters of this book distill the recognition of that essential purpose into a desire to assist preachers in their crucial role. Preachers are essentially translators of God's saving work to the people they serve.

And yet the difficulty that those called to preach often experience lies right at the heart of the mission to preach. In workshops and at retreats, priests complain that they are not experts in Scripture. How can they be sure that they are preaching *the* correct interpretation of the text?

In reality, the most common danger for the homilist is not that he will lead people astray by erroneous doctrine but that he will allow his faith-horizon to shrink into a purely human perspective. For this reason, I once again recall that the preacher must be constantly opening himself up to the Burning Word; he must allow it to give him the faith he needs to experience Scripture as saving power, as future-creating language.

In this way he becomes involved in the dynamism of the Incarnation as living witness to the new creation. Society's serious ills, the conditions to which preachers must now address themselves, are daily reminders of the need for great courage and commitment to trust in the healing power of the Word. Only this loyalty enables us to overcome the false dilemma portrayed in the once televised novel *Catholics*: either a fundamentalistic withdrawal or a secularistic compromise. A prophet must help men see the solution to the widening horizons that can bring deeper healing.

Preaching is a channeled ecstasy growing out of spiritual and moral insight and discipline. It is a special form of communication that uses the religious traditions growing out of biblical revelation to build up the community of believers. It is an exercise of religious language that requires faith to be understood and accepted. How often students do not accept some implications of New Testament teaching presented in class — Luke, for example, on poverty! And yet the truth stands strong: we do not discover reality. Reality brings us to birth when religious imagination illumines the images of contemporary society and through them once more lets the new creation bring us to birth.

The Dilemma of Today's Preacher

In an important discourse on exegesis and hermeneutics Pope Paul VI told Italian biblical scholars that fidelity to contemporary man is a responsibility of preachers and also an exacting task.[1] The fuller awareness that modern science has brought to the complexity of the human person and his precarious relationship to his environment, not to mention the ever increasing rapidity of severe cultural shocks that are burning mankind's bridges behind him, make the preacher's role an awesome challenge for himself and a necessary function in the believing community.

The Word of God that alone can create a world of hope comes to modern society dressed in the time-conditioned language and institutions of a foreign culture, in literary forms that are strange to modern thought patterns. The preacher needs indeed a contemporary theopoetic; he must be able to translate the text, to bridge the language gap, to reclothe the life-giving Word in terms that secularized persons can understand, identify with, and ultimately accept as liberating. The temptation to disregard the text is strong. Can't some substitute be found? The drive is strong to substitute process for reality.

Here the faith of the preacher is what bridges the apparently unbridgeable gap. He must show that the text provides a common home, a fulcrum for creating a hopeful future. Scripture is a privileged expression, an authentic prolongation of the believing apostolic community, composed near the beginning of the Christian experience to build up members. From the beginning of the Christian era it has continued to call believers together, to guide their thanksgiving, to promise them eternal life. Historically, every religious group has been called to spiritual fellowship by a sacred text. The Christian community needs preachers who can make the power of the inspired text radiate in their midst and in their hearts.

Scripture itself, then, creates the need for preachers who will assume the responsibility of assembling believing communities, address them in the name and power of the Lord Jesus, and act as his prophets. Along with Scripture, the preacher is constitutive of apostolic presence. Language is the extension of men, the symbol humans use to portray and share and interpret the reality in which they find their ultimate destiny. What is reality? Not a static, completed, closed universe, but rather the open, unlimited possibilities of the wisdom and power and grace of God. Through their language of faith the inspired authors created a world that expresses this reality and enables men to experience it. This new world was rooted in and yet transcended their limited cultural horizons.

Contemporary Christian preachers find themselves in a cross fire of conflicting tensions. Culturally, on the one hand, they are distant from the early Christians and much of the New Testament terminology but at home in modern society. By faith, on the other hand, the preacher is one with the apostolic belief but hostile to the diminished existence imposed by secular humanism. And so, he faces a stiff challenge.

How can he become the facilitator of gospel power that is making this new world available and so offering a healing for today's needs? If Scripture is to touch through the preacher, it must bring this light. It must enlighten and transform the preacher's whole being and situation before he can be the light to others. Surely, one reason why the Bible does not enlighten many readers today is because preaching of Scripture has failed. The preacher is darkness, confusion, doubt, ambiguity — not saving light.

Preachers, then, are called to be prophets of light in their liturgical homilies because this is the only preaching, the only religious language that many Christians encounter today. In theory, it is desirable that the homilist does not have to devote himself to instructing but rather to deepening already existing religious convictions. In practice, however, today's preacher must devote much of his time to teaching. If he does not know how to instruct on a truly religious level — or refuses to face this reality — he could be talking for the most part to himself.

In this explanation of the Burning Word as prophetic voice, I would like to help prepare the way by which preachers can perform their role as religious instructors rather than as mere imparters of information. I would like to discuss the qualities of religious language that form the heart of scriptural preaching. For, as Dupré explains in his important study of religious language, when an article of faith becomes mere information — out there — "it is religiously dead."[2]

Preachers as Instructors

The New Testament is that library of writings that sprang from and speaks to the unique religious experience brought to men by Jesus Christ. It spoke the language of men with a definite religious background and clear spiritual goals. The people in the churches who hear it read and explained today share only in a limited degree those goals. The education of the church-going Catholic does not prepare him to think religiously. Religious language has become the speciality of an elite.[3]

As religious literature, the writings of the New Testament seek to involve, to create new horizons, to demand commitment. To illustrate these three aims: the New Testament involves us by calling God "Father"; it creates new horizons by calling another person "brother"; it demands commitment by calling us to be reconciled to God.

Without going into theories of language or of learning, the preacher must at least appreciate the gap existing between his hearers and the liturgical text he proclaims. He must bridge this gap quickly in a homily because time is short. It takes imagination and skill to transport hearers from the morning newspaper,

from last night's TV special, from a family quarrel, or
whatever the distraction, to the biblical text he has
just proclaimed. He can effect this miracle only by his
personal appreciation of the message, his faith commitment to it, and his ability to bring it into the consciousness of his hearers.

All of this means that the preacher must prepare.
Seminary formation is obviously only a remote preparation. A broad liberal arts foundation, the ability to
handle philosophical reasoning, even systematic
theological reflection do not automatically create a
preacher. A preacher has to know how language
works. Where do sentences come from? And where
do they go? But something more is needed: his own
personal study and experience of the text chosen for
the celebration.

Here the preacher faces a critical decision. Is he willing to wrestle with the text and be interpreted by it?
The pulpit is not the place to play the game of scientific exegesis; that struggle must go on beforehand. In
fact, that is part of the "Be attentive" of Lonergan's
first transcendental.[4]

What method can the preacher use to make himself
more familiar with the biblical text? Of the many possibilities, one effective tool that is easy to use is *semantic paraphrase*. I have appended to this chapter some
basics of such paraphrasing. What is the advantage of
the semantic paraphrase? It helps the preacher to become contemporary with the sacred writer and view
the world from his believing eyes. It is like seeing a
coral reef through a glass-bottom boat. A new richness
of the world of language opens before his eyes, and a
variety of relationships emerge. When Ephesians 1:4
says that God chose us "from the foundation of the
world," the preacher sees that the text is speaking

about a religious truth. It is not a biological theory nor an archeological judgment. It means that our whole existence depends upon the wisdom of God involved in the creation of the universe.

By way of further example: the frequent epithet "God of peace" designates God as the wise and powerful Lord who alone provides what men need for healing and wholeness. The "incentive of love" that Paul urges in Philippians 2:1 designates *agape*-love as a force that creates a Christian community. The preacher would do well to compose a *semantic paraphrase* of that little preface to the hymn of Christ's self-emptying in Philippians 2:1-4 because it contains a whole series of intimate relationships that lay bare the relationships active in a fervent Christian community. An instructive exercise would be to take different translations of key texts and experience the impact each makes.

Meaning is Choice

The preacher who undertakes to lay open the significance of the Burning Word of Scripture does so, then, not as conveyor of information. Meaning implies the power of the text to move the hearers. When Chrysostom said, "The law condemned sin, but grace destroyed sin," he was speaking of the effective power of the Good News. And so, Paul could define the gospel as "God's power to save everyone who believes" (Rom. 1:16). Because human beings choose by means of their enlightened will, the preacher cannot ignore the affective side of the prophetic word of Scripture, which is a long process of religious persuasion. The prophets spoke to convert: "Return to your God." Jesus sent his disciples to preach "conversion and forgiveness of sins" (Luke 24:47).

The meaning of any passage is not simply its informational content, but also the emotions embedded in it and the type of response that the inspired author wished to stir up in his audience. The responsibility of preaching involves the effort to deliver homilies in a way that evokes response in contemporary hearers. Fidelity to God's word means letting it shine forth anew in all its freshness and power to create its world for believers today. The personal input is the role of the preacher as prophet: he is one who makes God alive now for men.

This fidelity to the word looks backward and forward. It reaches back to the original writer to submit to the Spirit who worked within him. But it also plunges forward to create a richer future for the assembled, believing community. In this sense, the preacher is as necessary as the original author as minister of the saving Word. He creates anew the word event that empowers hearers to respond in loving obedience. He builds up the Body of Chirst in love.

As he embraces this task, it is important that the preacher does not tie himself up in knots by fears such as the one I mentioned at the beginning of this chapter. Every liturgical celebration offers the believing preacher some beauty of the new creation that he can celebrate with his congregation according to the unique lines of his formation and experience. When he submits his talents and concern to the Burning Word, it makes him an effective minister in building up the people of God. The preacher's language can become adequate if he is willing to work through individual writings of the New Testament and, in the power of the Spirit, put passages into meaningful forms. Here, as an introduction, I want to present briefly aspects of religious language that play a crucial role in biblical preaching.

Religious Language

Religious language always presents a challenge to human attempts to cope with reality. Philosophy grew out of an attempt to reflect upon the religious myths of the ancient gods. Hellenistic philosophy was concerned with updating Homeric myths to make them relevant for sophisticated cosmopolitan scholars. The important question on the analogy of being (found in the first part of the *Summa Theologica*) tells how St. Thomas Aquinas indicated that religious language permeated every response he wrote. We forget this in our effort to control reality, forgetting also that we thereby diminish ourselves.

Every preacher must accept the need of using religious language if he hopes to translate Scripture into terms that contemporary hearers can cope with. It is not a question of becoming a philosopher of language or of being able to analyze theories of learning. Rather, it is primarily a need to avoid all forms of wooden criticism that keep well-educated persons trapped in a fundamentalistic attitude toward revelation. How can moderns deal with the apocalyptic language of the Bible? The recent letter of the executive board of the Catholic Biblical Association to the American bishops calls attention to this problem.[5]

What is religious language? Perhaps the best approach is to begin by eliminating what it is not. It is not scientific, objectifying language. By this I mean that men cannot speak of God in the way they speak of moon rocks, as some *thing*, as another item of information that does not touch their destiny here and now. On the other hand, religious language is not something purely subjective, a purely personal universe each person creates for himself cut off from contact with the real world.

In a positive vein, religious language is self-involving discourse. Any statement toward the personal Father who shows himself as reconciling in Jesus Christ is necessarily a statement about man, about his relationship to the universe, about his history, about his destiny, about what justifies his existence. Because it is self-involving, religious language aims at commitment, persuasion, conversion. It warns, offers hope, places man under judgment; it instructs to move and to transform. When the believer says, "I acknowledge Jesus Christ as my Lord," he is pledging himself even more totally than the man who says to a woman, "I take you as my wife." When man invokes God, life is changed.

The preacher as prophet wields the two-edged sword that "penetrates and divides soul and spirit, joints and marrow" (Heb. 4:12). The responsibility of the preacher is to persuade men to accept this word that changes the direction of their lives by enlarging their horizons until they open up upon the fullness of divine reality. He attacks that "world" which John speaks against in his gospel, the vision of reality that embodies a living lie. This "world" is the mentality that usurps the place of divine reality and tries to shut out the transcendent demands of God. Religious language is the speech that ushers men into the realm of reality, the total ongoing experience of the Father's healing in Jesus. The preacher with the prophetic voice that is essential to him cannot allow the faith-vision to shrink.

Even as it is spoken, religious language is creating new horizons, new possibilities. At the same time, it plunges believers into new tensions, into the paradox of mystery, which is inexhaustible truth. How is such an experience possible? Because religious language when nourished by faith is life-giving. Reflective religious language is called "theology," that is, "God becoming discourse." But theology is built on theopoetic. "Before the message there must be the vision."[6] In it, God involves himself in man's destiny and involves the believer in the endless possibilities of his own infinite reality.

Without taking believers out of time and space, religious language shows them that their existence is not hemmed by these dimensions but has wider horizons. It is these wider horizons that prophetic preaching opens up. The particular form of religious language used by the Christian preacher is that rooted in the religious experience of Jesus and his personal disciples, and incorporated into the New Testament. It is the language of the endtime, the imagery of eschatological fulfillment because the resurrection of Jesus is the Good News upon which the believer stands, as Paul affirms (1 Cor. 15:1).

In his Last Supper discourses, John expands the mystery of the glorification of Jesus as the source of our hope by contemplating the mystery of the return of Jesus to his Father. And the paradox is that this return is not a departure of Jesus at all, but rather the new presence of Jesus as the new world in which believers dwell. The preacher assures believers that a Christian life-style is real.

How can this New Testament language hope to speak to contemporary men? How can the preacher dispose them to receive this eschatological world that Jesus lived in and now shares through his Spirit? This is the reality that Jesus told us to demand in the key position of his personal prayer, "Hallowed be thy name." This is a dynamic plea for the definitive and transforming fulfillment of all the hopes of the chosen people as they longed for the striking display of God's power. The resurrection is not an offense to faith.[7] It demands in the believer a climate of openness to God's liberating presence in his life, in his cult, and in his interpersonal relationships.

Forms of New Testament Language

The community experience of the resurrection presence of the Lord Jesus manifested in his Spirit produced its own religious language. This reality had to break into language, and this language took concrete form in new literary houses, that is, in literary forms capable of celebrating and communicating the faith experience of being reconciled to the Father in Jesus Christ. The two major forms of literature brought into existence by this new faith experience were the *apostolic letter* and the *gospel*. Both are intimately bound up with the religious life of the primitive community to such a degree that their whole literary history was joined to a very short time span: to that privileged historical era when the personal witnesses to Jesus were still exercising influence. Since these forms stand at the heart of liturgical preaching, it is important that preachers appreciate their nature and their normative role in Christian life. In other words, they actually embody the creative power of the reconciling presence of God in Christ.[8]

The Apostolic Letter

Of course, Christians did not invent letter writing. But the Apostle Paul did invent the liturgical letter of apostolic persuasion, the authoritative witness of the chosen servant of the Lord Jesus to an assembled Eucharistic community. Through this literary creation the Apostle's charismatic presence became a language event that called the community back to the Good News. Through it the Apostle once more stood in the midst of believers to summon them to ground their existence upon the reconciling care of love of the Father in Jesus, summoned them to cling to the freedom only he could share with them. In these letters Paul turned back the darkness of diminished existence threatening young communities.

Paul always greets the community with a prayer for the *grace* and *peace* of God, those divine gifts enabling believers to be free to embrace the saving power of the Cross and to serve one another in redemptive love. The *thanksgiving* prayer that follows this greeting lifts the horizons of the community to the divine reality of the new creation. Paul then dialogs with the community about some aspect of the Christian experience and draws the ethical implications of their new condition. Preachers cannot communicate the demands and promises of these letters without identifying themselves with the world they create: not the physical, cultural world of long ago, but the faith world that alone enables man to become what he is, the faith world that enables man to enter horizons of ultimate reality.

The Gospel Form

As the first generation of Christians began to die off, the new generation of believers who had not seen the earthly Jesus felt the need of liturgical texts that would bring them into more intimate understanding of the religious situation of Jesus as incarnate servant who came to share their human condition even to death.

The response to this need was the literary form of gospel, again a product of that unique set of conditions that existed as the eye witnesses of the Christ event could no longer proclaim the wonders of God's action in Jesus. These inspired compositions still carry on the work of the apostles of bringing others into their experience of faith. They play a crucial role in accomplishing the beatitude: "Blessed are they who have not seen and have believed" (John 20:29).

A gospel is by nature a cult text, that is, a liturgical narrative of the historic activity of Jesus as saving event, developed in and through the believing community through preaching, prayer and liturgical celebration. Like the apostolic letter, the gospel form is a product of faith and a stimulus to personal commitment. It recognizes that narratives of what God has done provide the best expression of faith and thanksgiving. As faith documents, the canonical gospels, despite their simple style, contain profound theological vision. Those who preach these texts must first of all be transformed by them and wholly committed to them.

Of all the passages of Scripture, perhaps Luke's narrative of the Last Supper best provides the preacher with the prophetic voice that builds community. Around the institution of the Eucharist, Luke introduces a short instruction of Jesus to his disciples. It portrays their responsibility to the believing community. They are not to limit their activity to directing the community to worship God; they are to build up the community by personal service and by being witness to the healing power of God in the world.

To be a preacher means to embrace the world of Jesus with all of its demands. For this is to give prophetic witness by a living faith, by personal integrity,

by the eschatological quality of basic decisions display-
ed in a Christ-like simplicity of life-style. It is the total
direction that preachers assume, their effective quest
for peace and justice, their respect for life and dedication to improve its quality, their compassion for the
helpless and oppressed that proclaim the prophetic
word.

The activity of organizing the forces of mankind
toward meeting the needs of all people is just as much
a part of prophetic preaching as the study of theoretical principles of language and exegesis. It is in the daily
newspaper and the entertainment media that the
effective preacher finds concrete illustrations of the
demands of biblical language. Preaching is alive
when the saving Word creates a Christian life-style
among the people of God.

Appendage: *The Semantic Paraphrase as a Tool*

Psychologists and linguists recognize that the world
of human experience can be broken down into four
categories of meaning, namely, objects, events,
abstracts, and relations.[9] And so, a text that we can
analyze by descriptive grammar into nouns, verbs,
adjectives and so forth, can also be broken down into
these categories of meaning. The two main thrusts,
words that designate and words that predicate, fall
into four groups:

Objects — persons, places, things being dealt with.
These will usually be expressed by nouns or pro-
nouns, but not all nouns designate objects.

Events — actions, processes and activities that are
usually expressed in the form of verbs like walk, think,
believe, grow. Yet certain nouns may also indicate
events, e.g., faith, repentance, growing. If we seldom
experience the dynamism of words like "incarnation,"

we can be sure the audience does not immediately sense it either.

Abstracts — qualities or quantities of the first two categories. Abstracts are features of objects or events that can be thought of separately, like *strong* faith or repent *now*. In most cases abstract features are indicated by adverbs or adjectives, but this meaning category embraces such terms as *redness* or *be hot*.

Relationships — meaningful connections between objects, events, and abstracts. Some nouns include a relationship, e.g., apostle (one sent by another), neighbor ("of whom" makes this mutual), goal, identity. In most cases, however, a relationship is expressed by a combination of words, and here it is important for the preacher to alert his readers to significant connections. What is the problem? Simply that grammatical categories do not of themselves transmit meaning. And so, in dealing with unfamiliar texts (which is what Scripture is today), a mere reading is not comprehensible.

Let's illustrate briefly. The phrase "gospel of God" in Romans 1:1 means "God the Father is the giver of the saving power of salvation." The phrase "the gospel of Christ" in the Second Letter to the Corinthians 10:14 means "The Good News tells about Christ as the chosen Savior." When Ephesians 1:7 states that we have "redemption in his blood," it does not refer to the Blood of Christ as an object but as an event, namely, the voluntary sacrificial offering that Jesus made of his life to release men. Release from what? From their own sinfulness.

What we are stressing in the semantic paraphrase is a simple procedure: when we put sentences from New Testament readings into the categories of object, action, abstract, and relation, they often allow reality to burst forth and reveal its deep structure.

2.

The Preacher as Prophet

We have dealt with the challenge of preaching and the responsibility of the preacher to mirror the power of the Word of God in the life of the Church. This life, proclaimed by the inspired Word, is the dynamism of the risen Lord communicating his presence in sacrament and in the love of his Spirit. The specific function of the preacher as *performer* of the word within the community worship is to make that word become present as language event. Language event is "that transforming experience of the risen and glorified Jesus re-creating the heart of the believer."[1]

In the hearts of hearers re-created by the word, the Lord intensifies his presence in the Eucharistic communication and renews his new covenant with his community individually and collectively. In and through this worship in Jesus as the living temple in spirit and in truth, members of the community should be able to experience themselves as belonging to one redeemed Body. Out of this healing strength they receive power to receive one another and build each other up in love available to them in the Holy Spirit.

To accomplish such a transforming goal, preachers need to have a prophetic gift. But just what does this mean? How can we even describe it, let alone accomplish it?

One possible approach would be to examine the function of the prophet in historical perspective. In a work of great skill and detail, J. Lindblom places prophets in the category of *homines religiosi* and concludes that "the prophet is a preacher, a *forth*teller rather than a *fore*teller." Lindblom goes on to say:

> That which distinguishes a prophet from other *homines religiosi* is that he never keeps his experiences to himself; he always feels compelled to announce to others what he has seen and heard. The prophet is a man of the public word. He is a speaker and a preacher.[2]

The historical approach would then pass into the Old Testament period and study the function of the prophets in the Jewish community. It would analyze various prophetic vocations beginning with Amos, the pricker of sycamore figs, who was called to prick the consciences of inhabitants of the wealthy Northern Kingdom of Israel. A historical study would also have to deal with the various literary forms used by the prophets to proclaim the will of God as it applies to changing situations: oracles, prophetic law suits, symbolic acts, taunt songs, liturgical pieces, and the like.

Finally, a historical survey of the prophets would have to move into the New Testament period and study the important place of early Christian prophets in speaking forth the will of the risen Jesus and in composing the New Testament liturgical books, because these prophets functioned in the context of community worship, as First Corinthians indicates. In fact, one of the active topics of current New Testament study is the role played by these prophets in the formation of the New Testament books. Along with apostles and teachers, they were the most important charismatic figures of the Pauline churches.

As important as this historical survey is, it is hardly

the chief preoccupation of contemporary preachers, who want direction on their prophetic role.

Because prophets are "religious men," we cannot neglect the question of religious language, an issue that is becoming more prominent in the consciousness of all those who wish to communicate the Christian message.[3] For a prophet is the spokesman of the values of the community of believers. Leslie Dewart traces the current confusion in the Church to a language problem.[4] Without doubt, this is an area where those who are preparing to become preachers must become better prepared. Priestly studies need to embrace an awareness of religious thinking and its implications for religious education in general and for preaching in particular.[5]

While we must probe further the question of the use of language, I want to develop at this point the descriptions of preachers as prophets, a description already mentioned as one of the aspects of the preaching apostolate. I have described the function of preachers as prophets, saying that they are "witnesses experienced in the realities that underlie their common faith, men who are capable of translating these realities into language that touches today's world."[6] The two sides of their personality must be blended: personal experience of the other dimension of man's existence, but also the ability to capture that dimension in language. Prophets are communicators.

Prophet as Horizon-Maker

In contemporary terms, the prophet is a horizon-maker. He is one who lives in the awareness of ultimates and is impelled by a driving desire to push back the constricting horizons that imprison people and doom them to any form of diminished existence.

He senses his life as a service, as an enterprise expressed vividly in the call of Jeremiah, "See, I have set my words in your mouth . . . to destroy and to overthrow, to build and to plant" (Jer. 1:10). Because he operates out of this wider horizon of religious experience, the prophet knows that his life is going to be involved in tension.

This tension is of two degrees. First of all, it is against a purely secular vision of reality. This is to be expected. But the prophet finds that he is brought into tension also with varying degrees of imperfect religious vision, with a *do ut des* religious attitude, with despair, with hardness of heart. Some zealous religious workers grow discouraged and despair of pushing back the barriers of ignorance and malice. They accept what is as the totality of reality. "This is the way life is; people are not going to change."

The prophet challenges this vision of reality, precisely because it is unreal and he is a realist. He recognizes human weakness and limitations; men have limitations within their own personalities and within the concrete historical situations of their existence. But the prophet proclaims that what is at present is not total reality. Man's life is not confined to his own history nor even to the history of all mankind. Prophetic preaching eases this tension by its positive efforts to build up the believing community.

The Christian prophet proclaims that God has intervened in human existence and that God is "in Christ reconciling the world to himself" (2 Corinthians 5:19). For this reason, believers can no longer equate reality with what is. Reality is what the grace of God is doing for men and for the universe in the ongoing healing service of those who are in Christ. When Jesus, speaking in terms of the transforming power of his redemptive crucifixion, says that he "has named" his disciples "friends" (John 15:15), he was actually creating horizons of ultimate possibilities for mankind by empowering those who believed in him to enter a new dimension of existence. When he commanded his followers to call one another "brother" (Matthew 23:8), he was giving them the commission and the power to create a universal brotherhood and to give new dignity to one another.

The prophet as preacher, then, proclaims that the liberating power and presence of the risen Jesus is available as the dynamism of the new creation. Out of his own experience, the prophet invites others to celebrate this new creation. He recognizes that he, as well as every other believer, receives this new dimension only as gift by being brought into that overarching unity of the destiny of mankind in Christ that the New Testament calls mystery (see Romans 11:25). The Letter to the Ephesians is a celebration of this new reality in the context of worship and of apocalyptic vision.

Such a vision can be received and nourished only in the experience of faith. In *Prophecy*, J. Lindblom writes: "The conviction of having been called by Yahweh is an essential element of the prophetic consciousness. The prophet is appointed by Yahweh to perform a high task in his service."[7] Hence, the two essential elements that ground the preacher's role as prophet are: a strong faith-conviction, as a committed and experienced religious person, of being called to his preaching by God himself, and, with that faith-conviction, the personal conviction that the task of communicating his new vision is a significant privilege and responsibility to change reality.

For preaching does change reality. It creates new

horizons. The call to preach as prophet is a divine favor both for the prophet himself and for the community he is building. The prophet speaks to his community not simply in words but also in the total life-style he celebrates. His celebration flows from his call to be model and goad on behalf of God for the community. Called to stand out there as a voice — subtle or otherwise — to and for the community, called also to elicit from the members of the community the gifts and potential that the Word of God can evoke and develop in them, called to be at once witness and servant, the prophet has reason to celebrate life.

First Responsibility — Personal Conversion

The first and ongoing responsibility of prophetic commitment, then, is personal conversion, the living out of the new horizons he has been entrusted to communicate. New reality calls for radical change, total obedience to the dynamism of the Incarnation. It is only out of his personal faith orientation that a prophet invites others to enter into the overarching "mystery" of God's reconciling man in Christ. He leads them into the decision to accept the total reality of their creatureliness in the belief that they can become fully human only in the dying to self in order to live out of divine life as revealed in Christ. For the preacher as prophet is not arguing for some abstraction. He prolongs the historical reality created by God's own interventions for his people as interpreted by the classical prophets.

What is this reality that God himself created and communicated? It is the religious experience that actually took place among the Israelites and that is portrayed in the prophetic writings of the Hebrew Bible.

The prophetic writings are not neatly composed books. They are anthologies of oracles and sermons delivered by the prophets and collected by their disciples. At first sight they present the appearance of total disarray. And yet, read in the light of Nathan's prophecy to David that God would build him a house, that is, that God would make the Davidic line the carriers of his promises (see 2 Samuel 7:8-16), the prophetic writings provide the broad framework out of which the Christian prophet can build a world.

In the series of historical crises facing the descendant of David, King Ahaz, Isaiah urged him to live out of faith in God's power and wisdom and care. Even when the historical center of the covenant promises, namely, the Temple of Jerusalem, was destroyed and the king led into exile and the Davidic line cut off, the prophet of the exile, Second-Isaiah, was able to see the reality of God's promises. His prophetic preaching created the miracle of the rebirth of his people.

After the faithful remnant of exiles had returned and started anew, their high hopes were not fulfilled. Postexilic Judaism settled down to the drab existence of ferocious hostility toward the surrounding pagan world, a situation satirized in the Book of Jonah. The unknown writer of Jonah preached a conversion to the God of the covenant, "a merciful and gracious God, slow to anger and rich in loving kindness" (Jonah 4:2, citing Exodus 34:6).

The conservative horizons of the prophets gradually gave way to the future-looking vision of the apocalyptic writers who gave up on history. They felt that God would save his people only by a dramatic metahistorical intervention that would shatter history and establish the ultimate reign of God. The remarkable quality of this trajectory of interpretations found in the prophetic writings of Scripture is their ability to trust in God's freedom to create a future for his people despite the changing historical circumstances.

The prophetic tradition came to an ever renewed appreciation of the Lord as the center of reality and a clearer understanding of all reality as ultimately one in God's power. They didn't see this world as the center with hostile forces arising and divine powers intervening at times. On the contrary, reality for them was integrated by the divine presence that is fulfilling the divine promises in ever new ways.

The Christian prophet fits into this revealed tradition. He looks upon history as only part of total reality, a reality that has the nature of a drama that reaches a climax in the redemptive activity of Jesus, an activity still revealing its mysteries. His primary mission, then, is to bear witness to this interrelation of all reality as well as to the transformation of all creation in and through Jesus Christ. The prophet proclaims again and again, in the face of hostility, weakness, revolt, arrogance, selfishness and discouragement that mankind as a whole and each human being "makes it" in life because of the saving love of God re-creating him in Jesus Christ. As a result, the prophet brings his hearers to appreciate that all the revelation of God is "'for us and for our salvation."

Prophetic preaching does more than simply state this reality as a theory. It proclaims this reality in the biblical sense, that is, it creates it as a horizon of existence. Prophetic preaching is indeed *theopoetic*; it creates God in that it brings into his saving power those who before did not see. The goal of prophetic preaching is to "repossess the mystery of the Cross and its glory in a way that would speak to all of us."[8]

The insertion of the prophet-preacher into this reality is neither extrinsic nor arbitrary. He plays an essential part in the creation of the total saving work of God. St. Ambrose spoke about this long ago and used the gospel miracles of the multiplication of the loaves in the desert and the transformation of the water into wine at Cana to teach it implications. The way Jesus went about to work the miracle was for Ambrose a sign that the offering of life was the work not of Jesus alone but of the apostles and of the hearers also. In this chain of creativity, then, the one who breaks the bread of the Word finds himself in a challenging paradox. On the one hand, he is absolutely indispensable to bringing life and, on the other, he is not the cause of the life-giving power of the word in the lives of the hearers. This tension makes the preacher both slave and free — slave because he is free, in much the same way that Paul felt himself a slave to every person to whom he brought the living Word (1 Cor. 9:19-23).

Learning from the Word

The word itself teaches the prophet his role: full of power and yet powerless. Full of power to feed and nourish, and yet powerless unless brought to those in need. This paradoxical state of the word binds and frees the preacher: binds him as it binds all religious educators, to proclaim and serve — but frees him from the constraint and paralyzing fear that he is not effective. The word also instructs the preacher that he is to be its witness by identifying with it, by assimilating it in his personal prayer. His homily becomes a real multiplication of the life the word has given to him, and which he shares so that it gives life to the hearts of his hearers. The homily, then, is not an extrinsic communication of Scripture as an object, but rather the sharing of what has come alive within him. Scripture multiplies mysteriously in the homily and then continues to show its power in the lives of believers.[9]

The need of this history-challenging word is not less urgent today than in the past. Quite the contrary. The healing that Jesus spoke about to his apostles is always needed (see Matthew 18:15-20). Only the word can bring mankind into the horizons of reality that reshapes humanity and links the destiny of earth to the judgment of heaven (Matthew 18:18). In this sense, prophets deal with the truly revolutionary word.

A while back Ann Freemantle spoke on modern European revolutionary writers. She said that she had interviewed Auden before his death. He told her that he felt that his revolutionary poetry had not changed the life of anyone. In fact, he said that no revolutionary writings had changed history. Revolutionaries keep writing because the desire to overcome death is built into man's existence. Ann Freemantle went on to say that there is a difference between a revolutionary writer and a prophet. The prophet is able to see beyond his own cause, to transcend the present moment and thus to offer an enduring vision to those he serves.

The Christian prophet lives out of that unique vision that Jesus experienced and communicated, and still communicates in his Spirit and in the sacraments, the silent presence of the risen Lord. This vision continues to proclaim the possibility of escaping meaninglessness and alienation through the *performance* of the prophetic preacher. The Christian prophet, then, experiences himself as a real and necessary bridge between the self-centered, diminished, incomplete, broken horizons of disillusioned people and the ultimate possibilities God makes available.

The Preacher is Intercessor

A bridge is not an abstract concept. It is a living reality. This is why biblical tradition presents the prophet as intercessor. Even in destroying, he is rebuilding. Facing the people, he warns and urges and pricks; then, turning to God he makes himself vulnerable so as to attract God's presence to himself so that he can bring those he loves into that presence. We see this dimension of the prophetic mission fulfilled in the promise of Jesus to establish a mutual indwelling with his followers, in his abiding with them by the gift of his Spirit. Prophetic preaching is part of that abiding presence; as Henri de Lubac wrote, "The exegesis of Christ in its essential and decisive nature is not primarily in words; it is in action."[10] The prophetic preacher is this ongoing exegesis of Jesus in the community.

To accept the prophetic role, the preacher pledges to enter into this ongoing activity of God and to take it as the horizon of his existence so that his celebration of its elements becomes a language event for his hearers. It gives them the horizons out of which to understand and choose. Speaking out of his own prayerful experience of such a faith world, the prophet can encourage his hearers to assume their responsibility in it. Only this faith world tells men who they are, for it alone can open up the ultimate horizons of the mystery of human identity which is inseparably linked to divine self-revelation. Since God's unveiling of himself was climaxed in the crucifixion salvation of Jesus as his return to glory, the preacher as prophet must find in this mystery the integrating factor of his life and his preaching. To put this challenge in the words of Amos Wilder:[11]

> The special quality of the experience of blessedness or glory in the Christian faith is related to the way in which evil is dealt with. As is suggested by the term "Kreuzseligkeit" (joy in the cross), Christian celebration is deepened by suffering; and the early church's *hilarotes* or hilarity is possible without irresponsibility. This temper and the vision that supports it can meet the needs of those eventually disillusioned with other contemporary versions of transcendence or ecstasy. Perhaps the greatest single contribution that a new theopoetic could make — whether for the liberal churches or the evangelicals or for the many kinds of addicts of the Absolute in our age of Aquarius — would be to repossess the mystery of the cross and its glory in a way that would speak to all of us.

The mystery and glory of the Cross does not stand isolated from the total thrust of the incarnation and the gospel trajectory. This thrust is kept alive by means of the literary form "gospel," created by the apostolic Church.

Summarily, the prophetic preacher of the gospel must be aware of two factors in our contemporary society: an energy crisis and a modern enslavement. If we focus our eyes upon the first factor, we see that this country is on the verge of a serious energy crisis that will reach into the lives of all who hear the gospel word. This crisis is going to create new problems, problems that never existed in all history; and what God's will is in the new situation will not be immediately evident. An important part, then, of prophetic preaching in the coming years will be the responsibility of serious study to understand the issues involved in order to help Christians make the honest choices that will be necessary. We must make these choices out of the light of Jesus' own commandment of loving one another as he has loved us in the self-giving of the Cross (John 13:34-35). Preachers have to proclaim this command as life-giving and creative, and say "no" to unreality.

If we focus a little upon the second factor, we see that every person is to some extent enslaved, and this condition means that people have developed all kinds of defense mechanisms that are, consciously or unconsciously, blocking out the new world and new horizons that the prophet-preacher is trying to develop in them. The prophet must know how to live with incomprehension, misunderstanding, deliberate misinterpretation. At the same time, he has to become as competent as possible in how to communicate. That growth in competence is an ongoing responsibility requiring both long-term and short-term efforts. The whole area of developing a method of communicating the realities by which we live our faith and love and hope is a necessary preoccupation of the preacher.

To meet this challenge, I recommend a serious effort to interiorize a personal theological method. For this purpose, we have the mind-blowing work of Bernard Lonergan.[12] This is not a theology text but a method of acquiring a competency in letting "God become language." This method does not work in the abstract but operates from where people are. Lonergan begins with the fact that humans operate in an ongoing rhythm of growth and this growth takes the form of an ever-climbing spiral of the dialectic between being and becoming, between what is and what can be, between the indicative and imperative. Life is growth. And he expresses this growth in the form of a call to various *conversions*, openings to richer horizons. The rhythm rises from the following built-in dialectic of life:

experience (be attentive);

understanding (be intelligent);

judgment (be reasonable/reflective);

choice (be responsible);

and always in the dynamism of grace (be in love).

Such is the dynamism of reality as seen by faith. The Christian preacher as prophet keeps this dynamism vibrant and so becomes a healing force in the saving work of Jesus.

3.
Accepting the Language Challenge

What is my role as "evangelizer," as preacher of the Good News? One thing that the Christian homilist does not have to worry about is having nothing to preach about, because the very nature of his task is to create a world. Through the language of faith he undertakes to help his hearers share that mysterious experience which opens up for them a world in which they can move around and grow and search for transcendent self-fulfilment. All that I will say about "Sacred Scripture in Liturgical Preaching" assumes that preaching is a special form of communication using the religious traditions available in the Bible to build up the community of believers. It assumes also that "all religious speech requires *faith* for its understanding."[1]

Historically, we have noted, every religious community has been called to worship and fellowship by a sacred text. The preacher is the community agent who helps the word of the text bring understanding to his hearers so that they may celebrate the life it promises. The sacred text that we as Christian preachers use is the religious library of the primitive Christian community. It is divided into the writings that the early Christians accepted from the contemporary Jewish community plus the additional collection of twenty-seven small works called the New Testament.

This New Testament is really a little library of writings that range from one page to about fifty-five pages, composed over two generations by an unknown number of Christians. From a purely historical viewpoint, the remarkable thing about this collection is that it produced a revolution in book production. Parts of it were copied more often than any book in antiquity, and its use by the many small Christian communities that arose brought about the triumph of the codex, the handy book that we still use over the bulky scrolls retained by the Jews in their liturgy. Christians chose to use their library rather than enshrine it like a Torah scroll.

These writings continue to call believing communities together, continue to give to preachers the responsibility of announcing its message, for language is the symbol we use to interpret the world that provides the ultimate dimensions of our existence. Through this language of their faith, believing authors opened up a world of faith that was rooted in and yet transcended their own cultural limitations. Contemporary readers of the New Testament face the tension of being drawn by the message of faith and hope and yet repelled by the cultural distance separating them from the early Christians.

And so the modern preacher does face a stiff challenge: to become a facilitator of the message so that it can teach and touch. In facing that challenge, it is important to recall once more that all of our preaching arises out of the language home the Bible has built for us. This home has been enlarged and furnished by doctrinal development and moral growth, but it is still our home and heritage.

Before Scripture can touch, it must enlighten. In fact, however, the New Testament often does not cast light when it is read today. And so, we preachers must face the responsibility of being instructors by means of liturgical homilies, because this is the only religious language that many Christians encounter today. If we don't know how to instruct and don't work at it, what are we effectively doing? Here, then, I would like to point out briefly some obstacles we preachers have to face as religious instructors; then I would like to offer a method dealing with New Testament texts that has been successful in opening these texts up to modern men.

Obstacles to the Message

The New Testament is a set of writings that springs from and speaks to a transforming religious experience; it appeals to persons whose lives had definite spiritual horizons. Persons hearing it read or explained today do not live within that same spiritual worldview. The education of modern man does not prepare him to think religiously. In practice, if not in theory, the religious dimension of man is repudiated. Unless the preacher speaks clearly on the semantic level as well as on the physical level, he will not overcome psychological blocks. The level of my initial response to the contemporary preacher's difficulty is pedestrian but important.

The problem faced by the preacher or by the biblical translator has been expressed in the form of an equation by Eugene A. Nida, the American Bible Society's authority on translation (in an article, "Implications of Contemporary Linguistics for Biblical Scholarship"[2]). The equation reads $M = d \times l$: Message equals difficulty times length. In other words, there is a limit in what one can communicate, in the total message, the total meaning or information load plus the emotional load that a text or sermon can carry. This limit demands a relationship between the informed discourse and needed redundancy. Just what does this equation mean for a preacher? It means that the audience cannot absorb the message of the text or the explanation as fast as those who first heard Paul speak or listened to the gospels being read in the early community liturgy.

Consequently, unless there is some support from the homilist, the modern audience gets a muffled reception. The "d" of the equation is the static, the circuit-breaking noise that hinders understanding. It can come either from the richness or style of the text itself, or from the speaker — even in his diction, or from subjective factors in the hearer, such as his lack of knowing the background, his lack of interest, his daydreams and preoccupations, even bad weather. For a parent, a small child playing or crying is a distraction.

An important part of preaching, then, is to slow down and adapt the information flow. We do this by re-creating the original setting of the passage, supplying necessary background, breaking up complex ideas into simpler expressions, filling in gaps, clarifying relations. All these things clear up the static. Linguists have devised a test to see if the message is flowing freely in a translation: it is called the *Cloze technique*. It consists simply of leaving every fifth word blank and asking readers to fill in the missing words. This has been tried also on sermons, and has shown that at times preachers are really talking to themselves.

As modern men, who have to learn in order to preach, we also do not get the total richness of the biblical message. And this means that we have to prepare to preach. Seminary preparation is indeed remote preparation for preaching, from the broadening liberal arts formation through training in philosophical reasoning and on to systematic theological reflection. But all of this is no more than background.

The preacher must bring this light to his personal experience of the specific biblical text chosen for the homily. This, I cannot say strongly enough, is the crucial question: Is the preacher willing to wrestle with the text? It may be that exegesis done in the seminary turned us off because it seemed like needless hair-splitting. Whatever the case, for the man who has never developed a methodology, perhaps the efforts of biblical translators can provide a technique for doing the necessary implicit exegesis that is involved in preaching a text.

A Method in Preparing for Preaching

This method calls for becoming acquainted with the text by making from it a semantic paraphrase. I do not mean the boring practice of putting the text into your own words, a practice that is extremely subjective, that would be insulting to most congregations, and that is calculated to increase static because it encourages daydreaming. No, semantic paraphrasing is the method of breaking through the surface structure and restating the message in its simplest kernel form, that is, in the form that reveals rather than hides the meaning of each phrase. Such paraphrasing shows how the passage is moving because it is based on the dynamism of language. This technique, called *transformational grammar*, is used by modern translators to put the Bible into meaningful forms in new languages, that is, to translate syntactical structure into meaning structures.

If we approach the text simply from the grammatical

structure in which we have always read it (viz., the
structure of nouns and verbs and phrases and clauses
and sentences), it may appear insipid and deaden a
man's enthusiasm. But if we take a new approach and
search out the semantic structure, that is, the *meaning
structure* or deep structure, we are in a much better
position to find it full of surprises that can be shared
with the audience. We are not tempted to think that
preparing a sermon is a waste of time when we gain
new insights from the effort.

The meaning of the text involves not simply its information, what the words denote in this context, but
also its feeling, its emotion, its implications or what it
connotes. The meaning structure is not so much on the
level of syntax (viz., what does the text say), but "How
does the text cut?" "What choice does the text demand?" The "deep structure" uncovers relationships
between values and emotions and ideas that uncover
the ultimate choices called for by the text.

As preachers we must be willing to take the text
seriously, to spend time coming to know it, to practice
how to articulate its message and beauty and choices.
This is *celebrating* a text. Some will be heavy with insight; some will vibrate with hope; others will be stern
with warning. Some will push and others will attract.
Some speak to man's inner needs and open the heart
to accept God's grace.

Part of preaching will be the decision as to how
much one can cover. Should the preacher concentrate
on one of the readings or try to orchestrate one reading
by another? That decision is best determined by the
extent and clarity of the message. As an example of a
difficult text filled with semantic problems we might
consider the second reading of the fifth Sunday of
Easter, cycle A. The text is the key passage of First

Peter 2:4-9 (actually verse 10 is part of this pericope). The passage not only has many dense and difficult phrases (living stones, edifice of spirit, holy priesthood, put one's faith in), but it has the added challenge that the message is expressed in figurative language from the Old Testament.

The phrase "living stones" is object + event + abstract = members who support the community. "Edifice of spirit" is the community as created by the activity of the Holy Spirit; that is, it indicates the goal of the Spirit's activity, and so event plus object plus relation becomes an extremely dynamic expression. To treat a text like this, the preacher has to know where his audience is, and how much they can absorb. If he finds that a text is not communicating, he would do well indeed to try this process. He would also do well, I think, to be alert for examples in the leading prayer.

Once he becomes familiar with the semantic components and thus knows what the passage means, the preacher begins the process of semantic paraphrasing, of putting the text into the language field of his audience. This is best done by "back transformation," that is, by putting the passage into its *kernels*, its basic meaning structures, the building blocks out of which he will construct his homily.[3] But the mere analysis of a passage like that of First Peter is only the first step toward constructing a homily; it is part of preparing. We have to synthesize, to fit the text into its context in the letter, to see how it springs from what came before and how it leads to what follows; we have to see its own inner dynamism.

In addition, it is important to know what type of literature the letter is. The numerous allusions to the Old Testament and to the theme of God's special call

that created a specially endowed people indicate that
this is a cultic text, a text meant to instruct and exhort.
Here, we are dealing with a text that is itself a biblical
homily, a text that is both for the instruction and the
encouragement of the people. We note that the text
does not deal with worship in a vacuum; it integrates
response to God into the whole life-style of a people
presented as "offering spiritual sacrifices."

As a worshiping community they are also a witness
to the world of God's mighty presence. The text,
then, is rich, and the preacher will have to make a
choice of how he is going to use it in his own
presentation, how to speak to the particular group
present before him. Whether he builds his homily on
one or two or three texts is not important. It is important to concentrate on one thing and zero in on it.

Another passage will require a different synthesis.
If, for example, the sacred text narrates a miracle of
Jesus, the preacher has other challenges. Miracle
stories imply a world model far different from the
outlook of modern man. In an age when men can
voyage to the moon, when engineers can demolish a
high-rise apartment complex in ten seconds, the simple healings of the gospels are not all that compelling.
And yet, penetrating beyond the level of miraculous
relief for the sick, the preacher has the challenge of
presenting the miracle stories as revelations of how
God does break into men's lives and saves those who
trust in him from hostile situations. The gospel miracles remain compelling calls to conversion, compelling calls to effect a reversal of values, to seek a new
orientation of life.

The preacher must instruct, but it is obvious that
his role is not confined to offering information. As

noted above, the meaning of a text involves more than information. Meaning includes the moving power of a passage. And so, it is good to speak here about the preacher's role of homilist in communicating the persuasive power of the biblical text. Having dealt with a technique of communicating the denotation or referential meaning of a text, it is good now to treat the second aspect of the preacher's exegetical task: the method of conveying the connotation of a text, its feelings and attraction, its emotional impact.

Evoking Equivalent Emotional Response

Here, to a large extent, the preacher is left to his own sensitivity because, as the ancient adage says, "You can't argue about taste." With the increasing rapidity of change brought about by instant communication, lightning-like fads, overnight heroes, popular songs, it is impossible to measure the emotional impact of words and expressions. Like clothes, some words are acceptable in one framework and not in another. How does the preacher find out? Chiefly by observation, by watching reaction, by trusting his own heart.

This part of the sermon cannot be ignored, because a person's effectiveness as a preacher is his ability to create a new reality, a new world. The prophets spoke to convert. Jesus sent his disciples to preach "conversion and forgiveness of sins" (Luke 24:47). Knowledge of a text, then, implies appreciation for the horizons, values and emotions embedded in the passage and the type of response that the author seeks to arouse in his audience. The homilist has to choose his words and strive to adopt a method of delivery that will not distort the emotional impact of the biblical author nor raise emotional static in his audience. Fidelity to God's word is the effort to let it come through in all its fulness.

The challenge here again is twofold: first, to capture the depth of the emotions of the biblical author and then to be sensitive to the feelings, the needs, the blocks of the audience so as to structure the homily according to their emotional capacity to grasp and respond. As Nida puts it, this is producing "equivalent emotional responses" to the dynamism of the author's appeal.[4] This dimension of preaching is an art rather than a science. One method of developing such sensitivity is by comparing translations, because these are made for different persons and with specific goals in mind. We have only to compare the impression various translations give.

All of this, of course, requires practice, and perseverance, and prayer. Deeper dialog with the text in all of its dimensions in a spirit of faith and love and service continues to open up new horizons. With reading, reflection, and discussion, the preacher acquires skill in entering into the thought and experience of the various biblical authors; he can move around their writings with greater ease and familiarity and freedom of spirit. He will be able to draw items together in a truly creative synthesis; and he will experience the sense of being of service in building up the Body, of offering light to the confused and comfort to the hesitant.

Preaching is more than a purely functional task. A literary text is a new reality, a minor miracle, a work of art, an aesthetical object, a thing of beauty that evokes appreciation and response. To convert a text back into spoken language is another minor miracle, another work of art, another thing of beauty evoking appreciation and response.[5] In speaking, it is important not to overwhelm the audience with complicated sentence structure or confusing development. It is important to plan surprises carefully.

Above all, no one should become discouraged or overwhelmed by all the possibilities or all the fields he *should* know about. No, every text offers something that the preacher can celebrate with an audience out of his own formation and experience. When he directs his talent and interest to what speaks to him, he will be effective in building up the people of God. Fidelity to the message of the text will help correct his own short-sightedness and selfishness, and will allow his preaching to be fruitful.

Here it is appropriate again to note that the preacher fulfills his role as a member of the believing community. And once again, I suggest that the scene in the New Testament that best illustrates the preacher's role is Luke's presentation of the Last Supper. For Luke portrays it as the urgent agenda of Christian ministry. At the solemn moment of most intimate communion, Luke pictures the disciples as jockeying for power. Jesus uses this incident to show the function of the minister within the worshiping community created by the Eucharist. The disciples are not simply to direct their activity toward God in the worship of prayer.

On the contrary, to pray to God necessarily places them at the disposal of the community of pray-ers, so that they become agents of kindness, creators of fellowship, builders of the brotherhood. But this is not a closed off brotherhood; it cannot remain aloof from the human condition. The Christian minister becomes necessarily involved in the whole human condition. He becomes, like Jesus, a servant destined by

his total obedience to the divine saving will to offer
mankind the freedom whereby Christ made men free
(see Luke 22:14-30).

To take the task of preaching seriously, then, is to
dedicate oneself to living by faith; it means opening
one's life to prayer, to brotherly love and care, to
service. This is the celebration of the Christian mystery, the fulfilment of Paul's command to become
celebrators of life (Col. 3:15). A preacher cannot break
the bread of the living Word and at the same time
consent to conditions that deprive men of human
dignity. Honest loyalty to men is the part of preaching we often ignore because we fail to exegete the
word of Scripture, because we fail to look into the
New Testament as the mirror for ourselves as well as
for those to whom we preach. But preaching is more
than technique, more than art; it is witnessing to the
life-giving Word.

St. Irenaeus said: "The glory of God is man become
fully alive, but the life of man is the vision of God."[6]
It is the preacher's privilege and burden to help Scripture create the empowered vision of God that brings
men to life.

4.
Experiencing Bible Imagery

It is important to be conscious of the gap between the world in which the audience lives its daily existence and the imagery underlying the text of Scripture being read in the liturgy. The preacher needs a hermeneutic, a tool, a method, for interpreting the text as its various levels, for separating what must be retained as integral to faith, what is valuable theological insight and enduring wisdom, and what must be set aside as antiquated cultural baggage.

In the broadest sense, the Bible belongs to the category of religious language, an area that has been receiving more attention since the "death of God" period. That movement is in decline, but it has left traces. Right now, attention is being given to the language of resurrection. As an introduction to the question: "Is the resurrection an offense to faith?"[1] or, better still, as an introduction to the language problem that the preacher must face up to, I would like to devote more thought here to the nature of religious language. I would like then to zero in on some specific aspects of New Testament language and its underlying imagery, and finally, it would seem good for us to look at the cosmic faith horizons that support New Testament imagery in general.

Nature of Religious Language

Religious experience is part of human history; we have already seen that it has produced mythical language. St. Thomas devotes a question in the early part of his *Summa Theologica* to the problem of the names of God, and he uses the theory of analogy to provide the basis for God-language.[2] Every preacher must be familiar with the nature of religious language if he hopes to offer Scripture as the Good News of salvation. He must recognize religious language as "performative," as language that commits me to perform, to engage myself. Because when man invokes God, his life has changed. That is why, if a homily persuades one hearer to formulate a single prayer, the preacher has changed a world. Through religious language the transcendent Reality enters, breaks into man's world, uncovers himself, and involves himself in the destiny of the hearer.

The privilege and power of religious language is to open to men the other dimension of reality, the transcendent and transforming dimension that ordinary objective language cannot communicate. And so, without taking man out of the world of time and space, religious language shows him that his existence is not hemmed in by these dimensions; his life has wider horizons, and he must search for meaning in this greater and more real world. It is this wider horizon that preaching opens up to men. It is this horizon that he finds in the imagery of the New Testament, in which the Resurrection is the Good News upon which we stand, as Paul says in 1 Corinthians 15:1. John's Last Supper discourses interpret for us the mystery of Jesus' return to the Father as our dwelling place. When Jesus speaks of bestowing eternal life on his disciples, John comments that he is speaking of giving them a whole new world, an experience of the living God (John 17:3).

Aspects of New Testament Language and Imagery

The writers of the New Testament had to use the language that was available to them, with its genius and also its cultural overtones and limitations. In his study of the languages of Palestine in the first century A.D., Joseph Fitzmyer, S. J., concludes that Greek was widely used at the time of Jesus and the apostles; in fact, some Jews spoke only Greek.[3] Jesus himself probably knew Greek. The most common language was evidently Aramaic, and the Qumran scrolls show that a large amount of literary work in Aramaic was composed about that time. Hebrew was in use only in very limited environments. All the New Testament writers chose Greek as their medium; they chose the universal, secular language.[4]

Further light may well be shed upon gospel language, but here we are more interested in understanding the New Testament text as we have it, and this depends upon an appreciation of the thought and image patterns out of which it grew. These came principally from the religious experience of Israel, that ongoing historical and spiritual experience that created the Jewish Bible with its distinctive cult and life-style, "God's plan in its entirety" as Acts 20:27 says. This was the spiritual heritage of Jesus. Obviously Judaism like every historical movement had its ebb and flow. At the time of Jesus, the Jews were a subject people, able to maintain identity because of their fidelity to Scripture and tradition and their hope in a transforming, divine intervention.

Out of this tradition Jesus preached the coming of the divine reign through his own activity. God wanted to make himself available to men in and through his activity. In saving word and mighty deed

Jesus manifested himself as having a special relationship with his heavenly Father, as being an end-time
person, as being linked to mankind's liberation from
sin. Hence, in its deepest level, the New Testament is
grounded upon *eschatological imagery.* But what does
that mean, especially to people today? And how do
you convey this dimension of human existence in
preaching? It means that Jesus sensed God as being
especially close to him and in him.

We can perhaps capture that dimension by reflecting upon how Jesus taught his followers to pray in
the "Our Father" (preserved for us in a longer version
in Matthew's Sermon on the Mount and in a short
form in Luke 11:2-4). The dominating petition, "Hallowed be thy name," is a plea for the eschatological
fulfilment of all the hopes of Israel as expressed in its
cult and in its religious longing for the triumph of
God's power. This prayer is one of the major keys to
celebrating the imagery of the New Testament. It invites the believer to live in a climate of moral openness to God's liberating presence in cult, in sacrament, and in love.

Community cult is nourished by words from the
New Testament which teaches believers how to become an eschatological fellowship — one spirit, one
body, in Christ. These words teach us how to build
up one another in "joyful hope" for the coming of the
Lord Jesus when, as just judge, he will become the
personal reward of "all those who love his coming" (2
Tim. 4:8). This overarching eschatological thrust
penetrates all the documents of the New Testament.
The words are quite ordinary, but the underlying direction gives them a richer significance.

For example, even the most profound, far-reaching
statement of the New Testament, namely, "God

raised Jesus from the dead," consists of ordinary words. Yet, this statement heralds an event that has created a new world. As a divine, eschatological fact, the exaltation of Jesus escapes the grasp of perfect human comprehension, and yet, believers proclaim the lordship of Jesus who has entered into a new, integrating relationship with all creation. The preacher must search the biblical text for insights into the many-dimensioned mystery of the resurrection of Jesus as celebrating our hope and re-creating our destiny.

For, as a product of religious language, the New Testament does not simply tell us about what God wants of us. It actually leads us into his hope as its is celebrated by the community of believers. It is this faith dimension that the preacher must identify with and share. The New Testament writers were caught up in that interior dynamism of God working in Jesus and in his Spirit in and through them. And so we turn to the manifestation of that new dimension created within the lives of the New Testament writers by the experience of Jesus.

The Faith Horizons of the New Testament Writers

It is the process of entering into sympathetic communication with the New Testament writers' mind-set that creates the dilemma and the challenge for the modern preacher. The picture of the faith and confidence and joy of the primitive Christian community found in the New Testament is, no doubt, attractive. But is that eschatological model viable today? Can the modern person accept its horizons? Can it evoke concrete, existential commitment now? Can people really pray today? Since the world has changed so much, socially, economically, scientifically, psychologically, religiously, and since these changes are accelerating at such a rapid pace, can the Bible as a whole and the New Testament books in particular evoke personal commitment? How can the biblical preacher provide an expression of the Good News that will become a saving experience, a language event, for his hearers?

This question is not one of abstract speculation. Because of the tensions in the Church, a real fear of religious language exists among believers. In a seminary Scripture course, I have met the student who feels uneasy with a look at the various religious dimensions of the mystery of Christ's resurrection, afraid that any reflection upon the mystery, any alteration of the traditional language, would lead to a loss of faith.

It is vital, then, to examine the demands of the faith dimension of biblical language if we hope to present modern man with a call to identity and judgment and salvation. For revelation means that God in revealing himself tells man who he is, that his destiny is linked to Christ, and that faith, therefore, is a dimension of human existence. The question the preacher must ask is how he can help modern man to find a home in the world of biblical faith.

Perhaps the first response he will receive is a lack of interest. In the world of future shock, some claim that it is impossible to go back to any religious home because all is in process; stability is gone — and even undesirable. And certainly, if the Bible is looked upon as an historical and a literary monument, a small library of a sect from the ancient Mediterranean world, it could be considered a museum piece, a document whose hour has passed as an integrating force for mankind.

The preacher must experience more if he is to proclaim the Good News. For the Christian preacher operates from a faith vision, a conviction that God has done and is doing something new in Jesus Christ. Jesus makes God available to people in a liberating way, a way so transforming that Paul was forced to call it a "new creation" (2 Cor. 5:17), truly a new home for believers to live in and move and find their identity. For where does a person really celebrate life? What is our true home?

It is not the world of external objects, which we share with animals, and which we abuse so by our arrogance that we have our present ecological crisis. No; as human beings we live in a world of shared values, of common hopes, a world that can exist only to the degree that it is shared and celebrated. For the Christian, what is this world?

Acts of the Apostles, in its description of the first Pentecost and of the repeated outpourings of the Holy Spirit, proclaims this world as the sharing and dynamism created by the presence of the Holy Spirit, sent by the living Lord Jesus. The Father has given us to Jesus Christ as his own gift, and Jesus has acknowledged and accepted this gift by making his Holy Spirit the dynamic force in our destiny. And so we now know God by the very experience of our faith existence. Our home is that mysterious realm that Paul calls being "in Christ," and which makes us "sharers of the divine nature" (2 Peter 1:4).

It took time for this new world to impress itself upon the consciences of believers and to develop the language and the symbols that would give it identity for its own growth, for setting itself apart from others. It took years of experimentation, adaptation, diversification, struggle and compromise before the

Christian movement fully articulated its identity.[5] The twin pillars of this home were the shared fellowship they cultivated in proclaiming the Good News and the unity of their common concern and worship. As *Acts* says, the community grew by "persevering in the teaching of the apostles and in the fellowship, in the breaking of bread and in prayer" (Acts 2:42).

If we had to summarize the new world created by the event of Christ's coming and called into existence again and again by the preacher's proclamation, we would say that it is the world of "freedom from sin" resulting from truth (John 8:32), the world of "openness" toward God (1 John 2:28; 3:21; 4:17; 5:14). Preaching is a call to enjoy the experience of having God as support and companion, and of being called to celebrate this world in creative love that *our* joy may be filled (1 John 1:4), the embracing joy of apostolic community enlarging itself.

The unfolding of this new world produced (as we have seen) its own language. We have also noted that the two major forms of literature brought into being by this new community are apostolic letter and gospel, both intimately bound up with the experience of the primitive community. These forms create the horizons in which biblical imagery appears. Indeed, the imagery is so bound up with these forms that in coming to know the forms we are brought into the imagery and enabled to experience the reality celebrated in these works.

How can these New Testament writings fulfill the aim of stimulating faith today? How can New Testament language make a home for contemporary man, become an event that fires his existence with imagination and dedication? Sad commentary when people thrill to the performance of *Godspell* and fall asleep during a homily. The question is insistent: how can the New Testament writings convey today the power of the faith horizons of that early community? This is what preaching is for. The obvious truth is that, in addition to his own knowledge, the preacher must participate in the faith dimensions of those who composed the New Testament books. But how can he do so in language that has not become drab and tasteless and rigid?[6]

Advice from Pope Paul VI

One of the best guides on how to develop a method is found in a talk given by Pope Paul VI to a group of Italian biblical scholars, a talk we referred to briefly earlier in this work.[7] The Pope spoke about the need of a method of interpretation, a hermeneutic, to make the exegesis, the actual explanation, meaningful to people today. And he gave three conditions that the modern preacher must fulfill if he is to keep Scripture alive:

(a) the interpreter must explain how the message of Scripture applies to the present and is really a message of hope for contemporary society. He has to show that Scripture has something to offer today;

(b) the very person of the commentator is not outside of the work of explaining the message. The text must first interpret him and involve him in its power and challenge. Pope Paul speaks here of religious knowing: everyone who interprets Scripture is first of all interpreted by it, and must approach it in that humble spirit of openness which alone preludes the full understanding of the message;

(c) the preacher must find some common interest or common need with the passage so as to be able to identify with it and thus hear it. He does this by submitting to the same Spirit who inspired the text and obeying his gracious presence. Communion is on the deep level of the text.

In other words, the Pope makes clear that the preacher is the bridge between Scripture and the modern believer, and that he must be faithful to the demands of both; for both text and audience present a challenge. Preaching, then, is not a "cool" medium; it is a continuation of the process of religious persuasion begun by the apostles that once wooed the world from its pagan values. Today, some of the equipment that a preacher can use is found in the techniques of transformational grammar, the ability to translate the sometimes obscure sentences of Scripture into their semantic kernels, to know how to use objects and events and abstracts and relations to translate the biblical imagery into modern categories of personalism, process, pragmatism and existentialism.

Besides the knowledge to translate biblical imagery with imagination, the preacher must have the love to communicate it with compassion. His person then becomes the medium proclaiming the power of God's gracious presence to bring the freedom that Jesus said his life was meant to offer, the freedom that Paul celebrates in his letters to the Galatians and the Romans. In the commanding metaphor of biblical imagery, creation is for re-creation in and by the Spirit. If a human being is to make good, and this is what every person wants of life, then he or she must receive freedom as a gift inviting response, must receive freedom as the gift of response-ability to the transcendent Reality breaking into human life.

Perhaps the best scene to offer as a picture of what the preacher hopes to accomplish is still Luke's presentation of the Last Supper (Luke 22:14-30). For this is a vivid picture of the Christian minister's agenda. Luke has introduced around the institution of the Eucharist a short instruction by Jesus to his apostles. It portrays their responsibility to the worshiping community. They are not simply to direct their activity toward God in prayer expressed in worship, but to build up the community by service and the witness of love in the world.

To be a preacher means to embrace the biblical imagery in all of its demands, that is, to give prophetic witness by a living faith and integrity, by the quality of choices and simplicity of life-style. Their life-style, their search for justice, for the improvement of the quality of life and their respect for life, their compassion toward the oppressed and their willingness to organize the forces of society toward the needs of all: all of these activities are just as much a part of preaching as the study of the theoretical principles of exegesis. It is often, we note again, from the newspaper and TV that the preacher finds the concrete illustration of biblical imagery. Preaching achieves its goal when the saving word comes alive in the life-style of the community today.

5.
Understanding the Dynamics of the New Testament

So far, we have been dealing with the language and imagery of the New Testament as a whole. But, as we have noticed, the New Testament is really the sacred library of the early Christian community. It is rich in a diversity that the preacher strives to make available for celebration today in the Christian community. In facing his role, the preacher might ask himself this question: Have I made a serious study of any single New Testament writing as a literary and religious unity and tried to enter into it as my spiritual home and let it shape and interpret my life and direction? What provokes this question is the thesis that only when the New Testament becomes an integrating element in his own ongoing growth will the preacher be a person who can build up the Church. And it is impossible to celebrate fully any particular part of a book without making the book, as a whole, one's own. In other words, the preacher should want to memorize the structure and thrust of the book he preaches.[1]

Even within the larger literary forms like gospel and apostolic letter there is found flexible variety under the overarching metaphor of the general eschatological thrust permeating the New Testament writings, all of which look toward the final triumph of the Lord Jesus and our share in his glory. Each work starts from a different location and follows its own route, but any particular text speaks out of the total thrust of the biblical book.

We want, then, to zero in on individual parts of the New Testament and indicate some of the forces at work as well as some of the trajectories resulting from the community's history and writing.[2] The preacher must see the big picture because without an overview of the writer's world, he runs the risk of getting lost in the deep forest of individual problems, and of offering mere subjective explanations of particular pieces.

To live out of faith, it is crucial for us to be able to enter into an inspired writing, to find a home in it, and to be able personally to experience how it is creating horizons that enable us to interpret our situation and the world around us. But, since these writings of the New Testament sprang out of a living, growing community, the writings also share its living character. Members of the early Church had a keen sense of being called and formed and led by the Holy Spirit. He was their ultimate strength and authority and guide for he is the living presence of the Lord Jesus. Influenced by the schematic picture of the growth of the apostolic Church given in the Acts of the Apostles, we have a tendency to think of the community as uniform. Traditional theology and exegesis have stressed the similarity and uniformity against the errors of heretics. As far back as the fifth century, Saint Augustine wrote a long book showing that all the four gospels were really saying the same thing.

Today, on the contrary, pluralism is accepted as a good, and uncritical uniformity is seen as a defect or as a defense against the risk of creativity. Contemporary biblical exegesis, under the influence of plurality, personalism, and process, places more value upon

evidences of growth and variety that appear in the
New Testament. Exegesis has its fads; it responds to
demands of contemporary needs, and has the tendency to find ready answers in biblical texts for questions never raised until modern times. At the same
time, advancement in learning and contemporary
appreciation of the value of pluralism has stimulated
interest in the New Testament community experience, and it is now clear that a variety of structures
and theological emphases existed simultaneously
during apostolic times.[3]

In a sense, even Acts of the Apostles sanctions this
diversity by its deliberate efforts to bring all of the
blossoming communities into relationship with the
apostles. Scenes like the sending of Peter and John
from the Jerusalem church so that the Samaritans too
could experience an outpouring of a Holy Spirit (Acts
8:4-8, 14-17) are the means Luke uses to show apostolic approval for new communities that sprang up.
See also Acts 18:25-27, for the case of Apollos, and
Acts 19:2-6, for another splinter group brought into
full community-sharing by Paul.

How, then, can the preacher deal with this diversity and appropriate its richness to build up the
Church today? Obviously, he must make himself
aware of its extent and appreciate what it has to offer,
how it came about and how it developed. Here, then,
we would do well to focus our attention upon the
following realities: first, the New Testament as an interpretive process; secondly, the crisis in the old
categories for studying the New Testament; and
finally, the trajectory concept as a tool for coming to
understand the New Testament.

The New Testament as an Interpretive Process

The New Testament is not so much a thing as an event, the record of a unique community experience into which it is possible for us to enter by faith, sacrament, Scripture, and repentance. Our task here is to learn how better to enter the door of Scripture and identify with the Church's experience of growing in self-consciousness. Just as an individual grows by becoming more perfectly present to himself, by becoming more conscious of his identity and by sharing himself on a personal level with others, so also did the believing communities of the primitive Christian church need experience to grow.

Along with their mutual love, support and insight, they also needed the challenge of opposition, misunderstanding and division. Paul is not surprised at the divisions among the Corinthians; he tells them, "It is necessary that factions arise" (1 Cor. 11:19). All of these experiences provided situations in which the power of the Spirit could be better known and orchestrated. When the community was willing to accept and integrate those experiences into the "obedience of faith" (Rom. 16:26), that is, when they accepted the gift of faith and translated it into a way of life, then the members came to a real knowledge of what the Good News was.

It is interesting that when Paul wishes to exhort his favorite Philippian community to live out their lives in Christ to the full, he appeals to community experience — fellowship in the Spirit, soothing of love, encouragement in Christ — that captures some of the creative relationships celebrated by the community (Phil. 2:1-4). Writings that grew out of such relationships breathe the Spirit and are able to communicate that dimension of Christian life that only the Spirit communicates. And once this dimension is articulated in language, the language itself enters into future experience and articulation. No single writing transmits everything, but each supports the others.

Perhaps what I am saying about the New Testament vibrating with this ever growing spirit of dialog, sharing and openness can be stated in a sentence written by a religious person describing her own experiences. After articulating her experiences, she went back over her words and then wrote, "Each statement is only partially true and even as I write it, it becomes something else." This is the spirit of *tota scriptura*: Scripture is its best interpreter.

Each writer should be listened to as part of the total interpretive process of the divine Word. For the preacher it is important to dialog with the New Testament texts in such a way as to experience them as they become something else — when he allows their power to interpret his role in sharing them. In this process Word becomes event, and Scripture shapes the life of the hearers. In the interval from the time the preacher chooses a text for his homily until the finished product, that text has become something else for him.

Paradoxically, once the primitive faith experience was translated into language in written form, it became more universal and flexible, because then it was cut free from the enfolding control of the original witnesses. The moment of writing down what God had done in Jesus Christ was a decisive moment in the trajectory of faith. Once left on their own, the words of the text continued to invite contemplation, reflection, dialog; to create new reactions, to widen circles of experience, to demand new horizons of community involvement.

In other words, the message did not remain static; the writings were a goad to the communities where they were celebrated to grow in the "knowledge of Christ"[4] (Phil. 3:8), another one of those pregnant relationships created by the Christian experience. The role of those who communicate these texts is to enter into the dynamism of this experience, to live out the religious imagery so that they may proclaim it as a dynamic force to believers.[5] It is becoming more apparent that what is important is not simply what is said, but how it cuts, what reaction it creates, what religious and social change flows from it. A document can be written for one purpose and then used by a community in a different direction. Reflection upon the reality underscored by one writing generates new understanding, which may not have entered the mind of the author.

Today we see phenomena like exegesis and interpretation of Watergate witnesses, backlash, commentaries on the song "American Pie," or Magdalen's song in *Superstar*. We know that Paul had to intervene at Corinth because he was misunderstood or misrepresented. These difficulties brought forth his most personal correspondence.

The more the New Testament is studied in its living context. the more its tensions and diversity become clear. As the Church today experiences change within itself and is called to fulfill its role of reconciling a rapidly changing world, its educators, its preachers, must search the New Testament more carefully and with greater faith and creativity to show what options are open in Christian life-style. The restoration of the lay diaconate, for example, and the identity crisis in the Church's special ministry have evoked an amazing number of studies concerned with ministry in the

New Testament. Here, we want to look briefly at what New Testament study is changing from and what it is changing to. But first we must look at the older categories and ask why they are being challenged.

The Crisis in the Old Categories of New Testament Study

The older approach, and the one that still prevails in most studies on the New Testament, is the static, thematic approach: introduction that studies the sources of a particular document, the language in which it was written, its date, purpose, literary form. This method has achieved important results and has enriched our knowledge of New Testament writings greatly, and its gains are not to be ignored or disdained. But this method has its limitations, its built-in obsolescence. For example, the inspiring presentation of a biblical theme in articles found in biblical dictionaries or periodicals gives the impression that the Bible offers a perfectly logical and comprehensive treatment of every topic of interest to a modern believer.

Actually, that impression is misleading. The theme approach combines data from periods that are far apart in time and concern, and unites into one framework material taken from passages with different purposes. I do not suggest that the person preparing to preach throw away his biblical dictionary or commentary. The information these thematic articles collect for us can be helpful. But such an approach should not be the model for the preacher; they provide background for part of his reflection. Otherwise, he succeeds in overwhelming and threatening his hearers instead of opening them up to a message of hope, to a joyous response in God's gracious presence.

The static introduction-approach reflects and fosters a mentality that is alienated from the ongoing dynamism of the New Testament itself. In this method, Scripture remains always out there, a thing, a foreign object to which modern man cannot relate religiously. Why? Because it proceeds from logic and does not capture the underlying religious dynamism that the reader is searching for in the New Testament. The preacher must work on another level to expand in his hearers the other dimension, the transcedent reality that is the interpretive dimension of human existence.

This religious dimension is not simply another item added to human existence but a transforming power bringing men to see the real world available in Jesus Christ. It is a world that has its own logic within the overarching eschatological dimension of revelation. Pure scientific logic or the philosophical and philological categories upon which introductions are based cannot unlock the transforming power of Scripture.

And so, despite the great progress of biblical science, despite increased knowledge about the New Testament world and its background, despite the widespread biblical programs, the New Testament still has not become the integrating factor of a renewal of church life. The Bible is still looked upon as the domain of an esoteric few. More and more voices are being raised to face up to this problem.[6] Better methods of approaching the Bible are being sought: ways of pinpointing real concerns. One attempt to capture the dynamism of the Bible is the trajectory approach which we must now look at.

*Trajectories as a Tool for Understanding
the New Testament*

I use this word not because it is necessarily the best word or best approach, but because it appears in important and controversial essays.[7] No doubt this word will become more common in New Testament research in the years to come. At this moment, it will be useful to know what a trajectory method hopes to contribute to increased appreciation of the New Testament. I say "hopes" because this method is still evolving and must overcome certain defects before it will be widely adopted. But, at present, it is on the cutting edge of New Testament critical scholarship. Briefly, we may present its hopes in three areas.

The first hope of a trajectory method is to plunge study of the New Testament into the stream of Christian history. The New Testament is at the heart of the Christian experience and cannot be understood except as sharing in the lifestream of the Christian experience. In the fullest sense it was an ongoing interpretive process arising out of stimulus and reaction, out of need and push. The dynamism of the Spirit erupted within the believing community creating the need to communicate the Good News of salvation; the New Testament is a part of the total movement of the Spirit that cannot be understood alone. As the new world of faith spread, it confronted other movements of history and a variety of social situations that pushed early Christian writers into new literary forms. The New Testament gradually evolved out of the ferment it created and evoked, and incorporates the preliminary directions that these trends started and fostered within the Church and the world.

Thus, secondly, the trajectory method hopes to call

greater attention to the plurality of resources and interests within the Christian communities from the very beginning and throughout its formative, constitutive period during which it was coming to self-identity. From its earliest stages the believing community embraced a variety of groups with diversified backgrounds and aspirations. Trajectory analysis offers insights into the creative possibilities of God's revelation in Jesus Christ and of its ongoing power to interpret every area of human possibility and limitation. The Church of each age is part of the series of trajectories originating in the privileged moment of history when Jesus and his disciples changed the direction of human history, and the Church of each age must take seriously its responsibility to keep these trajectories true and free.

Finally, analysis of the trajectories of early Christianity seeks to locate the individual books of the New Testament more accurately within the total growth of the Christian experience. No existing New Testament writing contains the earliest form of the Christian message, and all of them were assembled at later stages of the community's existence, when the lived experience had reached the point of feeling the need to synthesize. But the extant edition of the books incorporate the process of growth without leveling diversity.

Careful study of the gospels, for example, shows that they are mosaics of community reflection and incorporate liturgical influence. The letters of the Pauline corpus show the experience of the Pauline communities from Paul's earlier career until the time after his death when structures for special ministry were being attributed to his leadership. The New Testament books, then, do not preserve the whole trajectory, but only snatches: "a fragmentary agenda." Whatever was preserved did not find its place within the official Church texts until, as Jacques Dupont expressed it, the Church had "clothed it with her own flesh."[8]

This lived dimension of the New Testament gives the writings unique importance throughout the community's history. Lived experience is able to embrace apparently irreconcilable approaches to a common faith. And so the ongoing diversity of the New Testament is a vital part in the Church's freedom to bring the Good News of salvation to life in every situation, and to become totally available to men as Jesus was. Ultimately, it is the lived experience of Jesus that generates all New Testament faith trajectories, and so we must look at his experience of God.

The Cross, Heart of the Good News

But before doing that, we should see how some of the important trajectories are captured for us in individual New Testament books, working on the principle stated by E. A. Nida who says of a particular passage: "The linguist would never, of course, attempt to analyze the meaning of this verse [Romans 1:5] apart from its total context, including not only the entire Epistle to the Romans but also the other Pauline writings."[9]

As noted before, the most distinctive trajectory in the New Testament is the form of preaching that eventually gave birth to the gospel genre, which is deceptively simple in form but extremely rich in theological and religious insights. The creation of this new literary form must be attributed to Mark, an anonymous disciple with a penetrating faith. Mark was the first believer to unite the various attempts to convey the richness of Jesus as Son of God into a unified language event. He did so by bringing the ministry of Jesus under one overarching metaphor, one theological matrix, sometimes called the "Messianic secret," but better seen as the "theology of the Cross."

Despite the continual efforts of commentators to analyze and synthesize and interpret Mark in static categories, he continues to offer new depths of the mystery of the Cross. This is not surprising, because Mark's Gospel is a religious document, and religious language can never be fully grasped in logical categories. But it is also a religious document based on the profound lived experience of Jesus and of those upon whom he had sent his Spirit.

The richness of this experience makes preaching, praying, and instructing a continuing necessity and challenge. Preachers are called upon to wrestle with Mark's insights, to help them come alive in believers. Mark presents Jesus on earth as revealing God's saving will in word and deed and, in this way, creating the crisis of judgment. The life of Jesus shatters the preconceived notions of religion and messianic deliverance, and brings his followers face to face with the folly of salvation through the Cross. Jesus is not primarily a wonder-worker but rather the obedient Son of man, the divine representative who embraced the Cross.[10] The Son must suffer (Mark 8:31), and as a consequence, so also must his followers.

This revelation of the centrality of the Cross is the heart of the gospel trajectory. It sets up reaction and contradiction; even his disciples fail to understand. The continued blindness of even the chosen ones becomes a continuous reminder to the gospel readers that they receive salvation as a gift from Jesus. Mark's warning not to refuse the Cross remains a constant need to the Church. Each generation of Christians must hear this message of Mark and affirm again the theology of the Cross: that God becomes saving message through the event of the Cross as a loving act celebrated in faith.

The preacher must help his hearers to take this word of the Cross seriously. Without this trajectory the Church would soon become simply another enthusiastic in-group, like those mentioned in Paul's First Letter to the Corinthians, who were saying, "To hell with Jesus" (1 Cor. 12:3), that is, we are men of the Spirit; we have the spirit of the risen Jesus and do not have to be concerned with the earthly experience of the human Jesus. The trajectory of the Cross is secured by Jesus who chose to send out teachers, who chooses to send out preachers.

After Mark, what happened to the gospel trajectory? We note easily that Mark's Gospel has practically no teaching discourses, while Matthew develops five didactic sermons, instructing the believing community, beginning with the famous Sermon on the Mount. Thus, Matthew has tamed the gospel trajectory to make it the Church book par excellence, the foundational book of liturgical instruction. In doing so, Matthew deepens the roots of the gospel genre in the earlier believing community of Israel by frequent use of the Hebrew Bible, especially by adding a series of ten fulfilment quotations.

These ten citations, each introduced by a fulfilment formula not found elsewhere, project the earthly life of Jesus as bringing the Jewish Law and prophetic experience to fulfilment. At the same time, Matthew links the earthly life of Jesus more intimately than

Mark to the existence of the believing community. For Matthew, the foundation of the Church is taking place in the very experience of Jesus as he is being rejected by his own people, even to his death and resurrection. These acts are separating Jesus from the old Israel and identifying him with the true Israel, the Church, with whom he remains until the end of time (Matthew 28:16-20).

In Luke, the gospel trajectory is modified to meet the needs of non-Jewish Christians. These people needed moral support and example to embrace the theology of the Cross. They did not have the self-discipline born from the power of the Law. Educated by the drama and poetry of the Greek world, they needed a concrete example to guide them in their new life-style. So Luke offers Jesus as the moral hero, wise, compassionate, open to human need, loyal to God, endowed with all the qualities needed to command and create personal loyalty. Luke's vivid parables provide the mirror for practical wisdom. In short, his gospel is the mirror of the Christian, a mirror in which he contemplates his model Jesus and responds to him as did the persons to whom Jesus offered himself, with joy and peace and generosity of heart, willingly sacrificing all for the kingdom of God.

In the hands of John, the gospel trajectory approaches its farthest parameters. He places the whole mission of Jesus under the overarching metaphor of the Word who descends from heaven and, after freely offering his life in a courageous display of redeeming love, reascends to the Father in glory. Through his words of truth and his act of truth on Calvary, Jesus reveals that God is love. John forges a powerful synthesis of the Christian worldview by developing new language patterns and by his poetic figures grouped

in a series of revelation scenes that can be called signs
or sacraments.

In this gospel, a "sign" is a literary unity composed
of a deed of Jesus together with a revealing word to
explain some aspect of the Jesus-mystery. In a sense,
each sign is the gospel, for it presents Jesus as Good
News. And yet, each sign offers its own special attraction, its unique insight into the reality of the world
that Jesus shares with his Father and offers to those
who believe.

For all this poetic beauty, however, the Gospel of
John is in no way isolated from the living history of
the primitive community. On the contrary, John is
continually interpreting the cosmic conflict caused by
the inbreaking of Jesus as it creates a split between
the old Israel and the emerging Church. J. Louis Martyn has shown, for example, how the excommunica-
tion of Christians from the synagogues and its matur-
ing effect upon the Christian community is reflected
in the controversy created by the cure of the blind
man (John 9).[11]

Contemplating this gospel, the Christian community is still instructed and encouraged to accept its
destiny and its responsibility of being in the world
but not of it. It helps believers to be open to the ad-
monitions of the Paraclete despite opposition from
the world's wisdom and value systems. The Good
News still calls to judgment; one cannot hear and still
remain in the old world of darkness because the Good
News is power to live now. The preacher of John
summons his hearers to live in Jesus without fear.

After John, those who attempted to write in the
gospel form offered only poor imitations of the inspired trajectories, and early Christianity is littered

with the remains of apocryphal gospels with trivial stories rather than challenges of faith. Yet the gospel trajectory is not ended. It includes all the reflection, comments and dynamism created by the reading and celebrating of the gospels throughout the history of the Church. It is into this trajectory that the preacher must insert himself to enable the believing community to pass into the world built by faith in Jesus.

Through the trajectory approach, we can trace the parameters of various ministerial forms that surfaced. Aware that the New Testament writings are particular and specific, we know they offer us only fragmentary agenda, and so we must attempt to fill in background and circumstances; we must generalize to the underlying operating principle; we must translate the norm into our culture. We must always be asking: "How does the text cut?"

The Pauline Trajectory

The earliest New Testament writings, the letters of Paul, present a charismatic trajectory. Already in his first letter, written from Corinth to the Thessalonians, Paul experiences and shares the sense of "spirit" as directive of community. And so he writes: "Do not extinguish the spirit" (1 Thess. 5:19). Corinth was a different situation. This was a charismatic community, with individual members enjoying special gifts of the Holy Spirit: charisms.

Writing back to Corinth from Ephesus, Paul lists eight types of members, eight gifts in the Church: apostles, prophets, teachers, miracle workers, healers, helpers, administrators, speakers in tongues. And he subordinates all these gifts of the Spirit to the life-style of love in the hymn to agape-love (13:1-13).

Paul sees the Spirit reigning through his gifts (Eph. 3:5); and he sees the apostle's role as "service of the Spirit" (2 Cor. 3:8).

But the community at Corinth is the only New Testament picture of a first-generation charismatic community. By the end of the first century, it was no more. Hence, the remainder of the trajectory is unclear.

We see the second generation as a period of crisis. Where is apostolic authority going to rest? Who will control the revolution? The crisis question could be formulated: Is the Spirit going to animate the human, or is the human element going to domesticate the Spirit? Paul urges the Philippians (3:17–4:1) to keep growing, and he offers as components of the Christian experience:

1. a community formed by the common experience of celebrating the Cross of Christ;
2. a community that lives as a colony dependent upon the heavenly mother country;
3. a community that considers itself as temporary and thus directed toward the return of Christ the Lord.

The challenge, then, is how to keep alive with this new life. The role of Church order is to keep the community vibrant. In the second generation, the leadership adopts two basic approaches and thus sets into orbit two further trajectories: the teaching trajectory and the serving trajectory.

Further New Testament Trajectories

We see the beginnings of the teaching trajectory already in Paul who speaks of salvation history (Rom. 9–11), of the need of teachers (Rom. 10:14); and we hear Matthew saying: "Every scribe who becomes a disciple of the kingdom of heaven is like a householder who brings out from his storeroom things both new and old" (13:51-52).

In the teaching trajectory we see an increasing appeal to tradition: what is handed down from the original apostles. The position taken in Galatians 1:8-9 becomes strong in the pastoral letters:

1 Tim. 6:20	"O Timothy, guard the tradition."
2 Tim. 1:12-14	"Keep the good tradition."
Titus 1:5-9	"Exhort in true (traditional) teaching."

This attachment to teaching reaches its height in the Gospel of Matthew, the Church Gospel. Here we note the role of the disciples, the special status of Peter and his role enshrined in Matthew 16:16-18. Finally as the climax of this Gospel, we have the great commission in 28:18-20 giving a revelation, a commission, and a promise to the apostles. This will be developed in more detail in chapter 8.

It is good to call attention also to the trajectory of service. To survive, the community must have a group of ministers; here we are at the cutting edge of tradition. The community was gradually forging its mature self-consciousness through its activity, specifically through liturgical celebrations in which it became more aware of itself as the Body of Christ and also distinct from the Jewish worshiping community; through the intersubjection of its members, a point often stressed (see Eph. 5:21; Phil. 2:3); through dealing with pagan society, which gave rise to a large number of problems about Christian life-style (baptism of infants; mixed marriages; eating food sacrificed to idols; sexual mores).

The First Letter of Peter speaks to the community as

a whole and defines its role (1 Peter 2:1-10). We have
here a priestly community which is to perform a dou-
ble role: vertically, to praise God; horizontally, to bear
witness to God's mighty deed before the world.
Hence, in 5:1-5 there is a special exhortation to
mutual support. Two sets of ministers are mentioned:
elders (overseers, shepherds) and "young men" (see
Luke 22:26).[12]

As might be expected, the writings of Luke, who
came from a pagan background, show an interest in
the question of church order and ministry. He is anx-
ious to link the contemporary Church to Jesus and his
disciples. Hence, he accents the role of ministry at
key places both in his gospel and in Acts. The Last
Supper (Luke 22:14-30) becomes an agenda for the
Church and for its leaders; the leader is to be in their
midst as the one who "waits on tables," and the
greater as the "young man" (22:26). Their position
will be to work to build up community by:

> a) honoring God in the kingdom (the new Covenant),
> thus making the Church a community of praise;
> b) assuring the celebration of the mysteries "in com-
> memoration of me" (22:19). In remembering the
> death of Jesus, the community finds its unique iden-
> tity (see 1 Cor. 10:17, one bread, one body).
> c) by their care for the believers who take part in the
> community celebrations and life. The social responsi-
> bility of the community is part of its order (24-30).

A key passage in Acts that points up the serving
trajectory is the appointment of the seven (Acts 6:1-
15). Different groups within the community needed
special services; therefore the apostles and the Holy
Spirit chose men for such social service. These men
were not actually called deacons, but Luke links the
existing minor officers in the community to this first

modification of church order. (In reality, these men did the work of evangelizing and preaching.)

Scripture, then, is a phenomenon with its own inherent dynamics. In the Gospels, we find life-giving truth that is both universal and unique. Witness to the particularity of each gospel are the trajectories found there. In Mark, we have cited the leit-motif of the messianic secret; in Matthew, we recognized a foundational book of liturgical instruction. Luke has spotlighted the moral hero: wise, compassionate, open to human need, loyal, gifted with leadership that inspires discipleship; while John witnesses to the cosmic conflict — in us, among us, about us — caused by the inbreaking of the Word of God enfleshed in Jesus. We have seen, too, in the letters of Paul, a charismatic trajectory; and, finally, we have focused upon those trajectories of ministry, of teaching and of serving, that were essential for the early Church, that are just as essential for the Church in what we know as the modern world.

6.

JESUS – Source of our Faith Experience

We Christians accept the religious dimension of our life as a gift, as a revelation from God. We base our faith on a free and loving act of God making his otherness available to us here and now through his inbreaking into history as it is centered in the life, death, and resurrection of Jesus. We believe that in Jesus, God becomes language for men, invites us to make a home in the world of his inner space and join in a true community of life — a life described so personally by John in the Last Supper discourses.

We could not reach such a status on our own; we can only accept it on faith. Faith, then, is a formative, a root element of Christian life, permeating and shaping its every aspect. In a revealed religion, there can be no purely academic knowledge of God, because God's free offer of himself as *our* God is accepted only by faith, and faith is response, search, commitment. Revelation is always "for us and for our salvation."

From the very first Christian writings, the letters of St. Paul, Jesus has always held the center as the integrating source of the Christian experience. As Paul wrote to the Corinthians, they must reflect upon their role as being a new creation, "completely from God who has reconciled us to himself in Jesus Christ" (2 Cor. 5:19). The reality and experience and gifts of God in Jesus must be the basic and constant subject of

Christian preaching. He is the divine Word become enfleshed, the event and driving power of the believing community.

In medieval theology this truth was expressed in the title given to Jesus as the *verbum abbreviatum*, the living summary of all the richness of Scripture. The revelation of God, then, is not a set of formulas. It is God's communication as dialog partner, making us his friends by transporting us to be "in Christ" so that he actually speaks from and in the heart of the believer, more intimate than our inmost parts, nearer to us than we are to ourselves. Jesus offers us identity as believers when he reveals, "I am the life" (see John 11:25; 14:6). How can this be? Jesus is offering himself as the overarching metaphor that gives unity, purpose and destiny to our existence and to all reality. Only in and through Jesus can man celebrate life to its fulness.

This new dimension of life, this transforming dimension of human existence that the New Testament calls "new creation", is a gift. It is new not in the sense of being simply added on or achieved by magic or human skill. No, it is an active, transforming power.[1] It invites us into the new horizons of living truth that open for those who believe. The Bible describes these horizons in a variety of ways, pointing to God as the caring Father who is inviting us to participate in his all-embracing plan of salvation; confirming us by images such as living temple, mutual indwelling, temple of God; drawing us to experience this gift by being "in Christ," a phrase which summarizes what God is doing through his Son Jesus. The human experience of Jesus is the most perfect revelation of the divine plan and of the divine nature as compassionate, holy, wise, and loving.

The centrality of Jesus is more than *what* we preach. It also creates the need for preaching. Why? Because Jesus came as a member of a specific culture that is foreign to our own special experience and far removed from the everyday world in which we live. As I have been insisting, the preacher must guide his hearers to Jesus as truth by translating the human form Jesus used, a human form tied to his own time and culture. While on earth Jesus was really subject to a particular culture and was heir to one stream of human history. That culture had its limitations, and Jesus, as truly human, necessarily embraced the shortcomings of the historical moment of his life on earth.

At the same time, however, Jesus was Son of God. As such, even in his earthly experience he transcended in his person the condition of other human beings. His very presence was to offer rich communication about his Father. John, of course, stresses this quality of the life of Jesus, but even in the Synoptics Jesus insists that only he can give a saving religious knowledge of the Father (Matthew 11:27). The entire New Testament, for all of its diversity and ongoing interpretation and trajectories, is unified by the religious experience of Jesus and the special presence of God to him and, through him, to us.

The life-style of Jesus is the most perfect insight into the life and will of God. It is essential, then, that the preacher be in contact with that experience and be constantly drawing life from it. This creates a challenge for the teacher of the Word, for the preacher has no physical contact with the incarnate Jesus who shared our humanity and experienced the human condition in an ancient culture. Jesus wrote nothing; and all that we know about him comes from a believing community. The New Testament was written by persons involved in the faith experience, all deeply committed disciples.

The gap between the historical Jesus and the extant witness to him in the New Testament is, of course, a classical problem in New Testament studies: *the quest for the historical Jesus.* Closely related to this problem is the meaning of the presence of Jesus as risen Lord to his Church. These two questions have occupied New Testament scholarship over the past fifty years, and have a decisive influence on one's role as preacher of the Good News. It is good, then, from the viewpoint of the preacher, to consider three things: first, critical tools for bridging the gap between us and the religious experience of the earthly Jesus, which the gospel genre stresses as vital; second, the crucial role of the resurrection experience of Jesus; and third, the experience of Jesus now as the wellspring of preaching.

Critical Tools

Critical work on the New Testament has forced commentators to recognize that the gospels, which deal with the earthly words and deeds of Jesus, are complex documents composed of a large number of small units that grew up over a period of time within believing communities. These small narratives were composed in the oral preaching as leaders of the communities looked to Jesus as source of insight and as model for their own lives. When new questions arose and believers were searching for a guide, recollections of the Lord Jesus were put into the form of short pieces that supplied a norm for action.

It was not until the need arose that this framework developed; and it was the work of the believing community to provide a setting for the sayings of Jesus. In German, these small pieces are called "forms" or molds. The investigation of these primitive molds, how they arose and developed and were modified and grouped into larger units, was the work of the history of the literary form school. Rudolf Bultmann, a famous representative of this school, finished his study on the subject in 1919. His work was translated into English in 1953 under the title of *The History of the Synoptic Tradition*. His research has occasioned a large number of technical articles on the gospels which are form-critical analyses of individual passages. These analyses offer evidence about the historical situation within the community that gave rise to the scene, and they attempt to determine what part of the narrative goes back to Jesus and how it reflects his consciousness.

In the discipline of form criticism there is both widespread agreement among critics and a great amount of diversity. It is a discipline that requires great competence, and so it tends to foster exclusiveness. Members of the club run the occupational hazard of talking only to themselves. It is not surprising, then, that in the face of the grave problems facing mankind, form criticism has come under attack as bordering upon the irrelevant and as dealing with questions that are far removed from the religious needs of God's people today.

What form criticism has helped us to see more clearly is that the early community was called into existence not by some new insight or doctrine but rather by a new activity of God among men, a new saving event in Jesus. It has established firmly that tradition existed before Scripture. Scripture keeps tradition living by interpreting it for the community.

Today, a large number of scholars are concentrating their efforts on showing how the New Testament community was committed to the task of reinterpreting the legacy of Jesus and keeping it alive as a way of life. The school that is concentrating more on theological questions is known as the *redaktionsgeschichtliche* school, the study of the history of the editorial process. Even here the danger exists that this type of research can turn into mere technique.[2] Critical study of the New Testament has produced the disturbing paradox that purely scientific studies often miss the heart of the message, and are in danger of becoming like an entrenched bureaucracy that turns in on itself and avoids the vital problems.

It is important, then, that the preacher know how to use critical scholarship without becoming trapped in purely critical concerns. He has an important role to play in offering the people of God a living contact with the religious experience of Jesus as the person loved uniquely by the heavenly Father, as the person who invites us to share in this love so that we can make our final home there. How can this be done? What can we hope to share with Jesus on a personal, reciprocal basis? How can he actually give new meaning to our life today? The answer must be found in the unique resurrection experience of Jesus.

Crucial Role of the Resurrection Experience

As a religious person, the real world in which Jesus lived was not the physical environment of ancient Palestine but rather that world which he shared with his Father. We get glimpses of this real, significant world in his parables, in his intense prayer life, in his radical obedience to the Cross. These qualities cannot be accounted for by purely historical influences or by any combination of human circumstances. Jesus was "the man who fits no formula."[3] In his book *Jesus*, E. Schweizer describes the uniqueness of this Son of Man:

> What is new is not that Jesus taught men to call God "Father;" it is that a people more sensitive than any other to the distance between God and man, between God and the world, were granted the freedom to say, "Abba." They therefore found this freedom to be a miracle, an incomprehensible gift. Only this one man, only Jesus, had the right to say "Father" — that is why it is so astounding for other men to share this form of address.

We look to Jesus not for new knowledge but to share that freedom to enter a sinless relationship, to share a new dimension of grace, supernatural love and faith. Faith-life is not simply an imitation of the truth-seeking, self-giving, compassionate love of Jesus, but rather a sharing that brings us into the very activity of God in history giving human existence its ultimate justification. Faith assures us that God is actually bringing us to salvation and sonship in Jesus Christ. Such a situation would be impossible if Jesus did not exist in a special way, a way that transcends this entire universe, a way that encompasses and re-structures the world of man. This is the way the New Testament community saw and experienced Jesus in his risen existence. They proclaimed this experience as their hope, as the transformation of their existence in their confession: "Jesus is risen," or "Jesus was raised from the dead," or "Jesus is Lord," or "Jesus lives." Here basically are statements of hope. And the question that immediately arises is: why did they express their hope in that way. What has the Resurrection of Jesus to do with my hope?

We see most vividly here the problem of religious language. These statements about the resurrection of Jesus, which fired the primitive community, have ceased to be understood as religious language and come across as merely objective statements, pieces of information that come to our attention. One of the chief tasks of the preacher today, if not *the* chief task, is to revitalize the reality of the resurrection as religious knowledge, as the power of God. We preach out of the power of the resurrection. We have to make people hear once more the Word as language event, as God becoming the language that makes a world. How is this possible? Actually, some theologians have given up on the possibility and say that the expression can no longer open up to men new horizons and hopes.[4]

Are these theologians right? Let us test one statement right now. When you hear the words, "Jesus is risen," what do they mean to you? How do they affect, touch and change your life? Do they interpret your life, transform your existence and destiny? Is your life a witness to the power of the resurrection? Or is this simply an objective piece of information? Is Jesus for you a specially resuscitated person, existing the same way he lived before the resurrection, just a very special person but still locked into the universe? If so, he might be admired and held worthy of imitation and amazement, but he would not be central to our destiny as God's people. When we take a hard look at the mystery of the resurrection, we are forced to admit that it is not central in our lives. How can we restore the risen Lord Jesus to the role of Lord, of master, that he held for the primitive community? To do so, we must in a sense learn religious language over again. We can become aware of this by simply reading the resurrection accounts in the gospels. They are quite brief and simple, almost like a little story. We must start to live once more in the world created by the language of the resurrection. This is a multidimensional world, and we have to bring these dimensions into our consciousness. Thus, the mystery of the resurrection has:

(a) a historical dimension. To experience this, we ask: What can I know about the event of Christ's resurrection?

No one actually saw it. No follower of Jesus knew about it until he or an agent of God disclosed it as real. In other words, the historical dimension of the resurrection does not begin until the divine initiative of the appearances. Until Jesus opens himself as belonging to another condition, men could not even know of his risen situation. But once he did appear, make his presence felt, and begin the dialog of hope with his followers again, then a new world came into being for them. Jesus bridged an unbridgeable gap and created faith, as seen in the wonderment of Peter (Luke 24:13). Historically, the resurrection narratives of the New Testament establish the world in which we believe in the resurrection; we find our destiny in relation to it.

The gospel accounts of the empty tomb communicate the essential features of this new world, namely, that in it Jesus has passed beyond the confining sphere of the material dimension of life and now enjoys a status in which he has power over the whole universe as well as the destiny of men. Man's destiny is tied to his relationship with his own body and the body of Jesus. As long as his body is in its natural physical condition subject to death, man is severely limited in time and space. But through his resurrection Jesus entered into a new relationship with his body, one that transformed his body and broke the grip of the physical universe upon him and upon mankind. In the resurrection event, the body of Jesus passed into a new state of reality that Paul says is beyond human possibility to describe (see 1 Cor. 15:35-49). The risen identity of Jesus is a new presence to us. And what God has done in and through the resurrection of Jesus is to set men free. He has given them new possibilities and a divine destiny.

The historical dimension of the resurrection is an essential aspect for it links the risen Jesus to his whole earthly life. Both stages are part of the incarnation event. As Raymond Brown said in the Brussels' World Congress on the Future of the Church: "Christianity would be quite another religion if Jesus had died of a heart attack on the shores of the sea of Galilee." [5] So also, if this same Jesus in virtue of his risen status does not communicate himself as living Lord, as having all power, as forgiving sin, and as sharing the Spirit of the Father, then we would be living in another religion and in another world. But this historical dimension of the resurrection does not exhaust the mystery.

(b) an eschatological dimension. The fact that no witnesses could recognize Jesus until he revealed himself places the risen existence of Jesus beyond the limitations of human history in the transcendent reality of God's life and reign. It is a mythopoetic or "theopoetic" event. [6] This liberated presence of Jesus proclaims the power of God to give men hope. The eschatological or "more" dimension says that, just as the Father brought Jesus through the dead end of death, so too in Jesus he grounds our hope. This dimension enables us to escape a diminished existence.

The action of God in raising and glorifying Jesus has already transferred our life from being hemmed in by the limits of earthly existence and assures us that we too have a share in the mysterious "more" that Scripture celebrates. By faith in Jesus risen we start to celebrate this reality. True, this is still in a hidden way, as Paul says (Col. 3:3), for the present. We live out our earthly existence in the "eschatological pause," able to experience the reign of the Spirit of the risen Jesus through our life of faith and prayer.

(c) a saving or soteriological dimension. We receive this sharing in the victory of Jesus as a gift of divine healing and reconciliation. In Scripture, the mystery of the resurrection is always linked to the condition, "for us," an event done for us "who believe in the one who has raised Jesus our Lord from among the dead — he who was handed over for our offenses and was raised that we would enjoy acceptance" (Rom. 4:24-25). God himself in free, creative and healing love has built a new world *for us* by this mysterious act that makes us gifts to his Son Jesus, living gifts capable of sharing his risen life.

The specific feature of this saving dimension of resurrection is that our risen destiny is a celebration of love and friendship that carries us into the very community of life that the Father enjoys with Jesus. Since the love of friendship demands a certain equality, the saving dimension of resurrection means that God himself becomes the ultimate meaning of our life, the complete revelation for men. The resurrection is the ultimate transactional analysis. God says, "I'm OK, you're OK."

(d) an anthropological dimension. The horizons of our existence cannot be enlarged by this gift of a transforming friendship with God in Jesus without a radical effect upon our whole existence. The resurrection involves a new self-understanding. It means that our life is not fully human without faith, and, in fact, the faith dimension must be the ultimate determining factor in our destiny. How we grow in our response to God in our relationship to the risen Jesus is the deciding factor that determines our life as successful or not. We can make good only in the risen Lord, "in Christ," as Paul said, members of his risen Body.

(e) a kerygmatic dimension. Obviously such a transforming dimension cannot remain isolated from our total historical existence. The resurrection experience necessarily implies mission, a commission to be a witness and sharer of the new dimension we enjoy. The resurrection of Jesus and his sharing of it in the Spirit creates the Church, a community of believers that lives so intimately by his Spirit and power that Paul can call it his Body. All of the gospels proclaim that the resurrection ended with a mission and thus continues through the missionary community brought into being by the risen Jesus.

The Gospel of Matthew is striking here. Matthew pictures the whole life of Jesus as the ever fuller sharing of the authority and presence of Jesus with his disciples. It reaches its climax in the final commission scene (Matthew 28:18-20), which is made up of a revelation, a commission, and a promise: the revelation that the risen Jesus has received all power from his Father; the commission to use this power to share the benefits of salvation; and the promise to be perpetually present to the community in its saving work. Believers actually live, then, out of this power of Jesus.

The Gospel of John pictures the fruit of the resurrection as the sending of the Spirit. But his insight into the mystery of the resurrection is not confined to the post-resurrection scenes. The long Last Supper discourses are John's explanation of the reality of the resurrection as the abiding, saving presence of Jesus through the Spirit-Paraclete.[7] For John it is the return of Jesus to the Father, but in such a way that Jesus abides more perfectly among men. Thanks to his new permeating, loving presence, we can now approach the Father in a new way and ask "in Christ's name" (John 14:13; 15:16; 16:23,26), that is, with an experience of his saving power and his glory. This new relationship with the risen Jesus produces within believers a transcendent joy that no one can take away (John 16:19-22). In addition, John sees this resurrection-existence of the believer as giving wisdom that removes any need for questions (John 16:23).

This, then, is something of the richness of the mystery of Jesus that we preach (see 1 Cor. 2). To be a preacher, to be a religious educator, means to be willing to plunge into the mystery of Jesus crucified and risen. We might say that it is the earthly life of Jesus as climaxed in his crucifixion-salvation death that tells us who God is, and his resurrection that gives us hope of enjoying God's life as our destiny. But how can this be?

The Indwelling Jesus as the Wellspring of Preaching

The crucial step in preparing to preach and explain the mystery of the Christ event is to plunge our existence in the risen Jesus and to live, in Paul's phrase, "in Christ." The absolutely necessary condition of Christian preaching is the identification of the preacher with the Jesus experience, the interiorizing of the mystery of Jesus, dead and risen. This will imply study not only of Scripture but of the experience of the Church and of the present situation of one's hearers. The key that puts all of these elements together in the life of every believer is prayer — personal dialog with God in Christ.

The preacher must realize that his task is, at root, a charism, a gift. Prayer is the opening of our life to that other dimension in which the gift is received. Through this gift God creates for the Church a future, because prayer brings believers into the sphere of the risen Jesus and makes them sharers in his power. This is the dimension of preaching that cannot be explained by pure science or taught by any set of rules. Prayer puts us on the wave length of the New Testament writers who were involved in a God-experience which they wished to communicate as a freeing word.

As the Second Letter of Peter reminds us, the prophetic word was not raised by human will but by men borne up by the Holy Spirit (2 Peter 1:20-21). And it is the same Spirit to whom the prayerful heart opens in order to proclaim this creative word. Through prayer the *verbum abbreviatum* becomes interiorized so that it can once more be enfleshed in Christian life-style. Through prayer, preaching shares the power of Scripture as a freeing act, an event that creates a new existence for believers. The preacher then becomes the true mediator of Good News, interpreting to believers today their existence in the light of God's saving will in the risen Jesus.[8]

7.
The Parables Speak to Moderns

The fruit of preaching appears only after the act itself has ended, when the life of the hearer is enriched; for only the hearer can build the bridge between the preached word and the world in which he is called to bear witness. The preacher accepts his charism within the community only through faith that the saving work of Jesus is continuing through the activity of the Holy Spirit.

In one sense we may say that the ministry of preaching was begun by God himself in revealing the first commandment: "I am the Lord your God. You shall have no other gods before me." This is a command only insofar as it is a statement of what is, an invitation to participate in the real world where God offers himself as dialog partner. The Word of God continues to persuade believers to participate in this dialog, to allow the indicative of revelation to become their imperative, to resist the influence of sin that would close them off from the availability of God in faith, sin that would weaken their trust in God through hope or cramp their love of God in obedient surrender.

The dialog begun by God himself reached new heights in the incarnation, life, death, and resurrection of Jesus, the most perfect availability of the Father. On earth Jesus carried out his mission as re-

vealer by word and deed, offering himself as sign of
the Father's love. All New Testament commentators
agree that Jesus preached chiefly by parable.[1] Obviously, Jesus did not invent the literary form of parable,
but he did bring the genre to a unique perfection of
religious language because of the way he used parables to introduce men into the world which he shares
and experiences with the Father.

Because of the special role played by parables in the
revelation of Jesus not only during his life on earth
but later through the gospels, it is important for believers to be familiar with them. Here we shall take a
three-pronged approach in our attempt to deepen our
understanding of the parables: first, we will look at
the history of the interpretation of parables; secondly,
we will examine the contribution of the so-called new
hermeneutic to an understanding of parables; and
finally, we shall study some contemporary parable
research.

History of Parable Interpretation

Within the very time that the New Testament was
being written, the parables of Jesus were already
being interpreted.[2] During patristic times, parables
were generally treated as allegories and used as illustrations of ideas related to God's plan of salvation and
Christian moral responsibility. Parable interpretation
was strongly moralistic; indeed, parables were seen
simply as moral exhortations in story form within the
frame of salvation history.

Parable interpretation took a sharp turn at the end
of the nineteenth century when the liberal theologian
A. Jülicher rejected all allegorizing of parables and
taught that the whole purpose of parables was to
communicate a single, personal, religious insight: the

"point" of the parable. This was an over-reaction that is now being remedied by the important contributions arising from greater attention to the biblical context of the preaching of Jesus.

In his important study, *The Parables of the Kingdom*, [3] C. H. Dodd showed that the parables go deeper than simple moral insights and are rooted in the overarching eschatological thrust of the preaching of Jesus. Dodd's insights on parables were related to his interest in the so-called realized eschatology, which places emphasis upon the gifts of salvation already available in the risen Jesus.

J. Jeremias built upon Dodd's work. [4] Thanks to his expertise in the language and customs of Palestine during the first century of the Christian era, Jeremias was able to offer important contributions to the understanding of the parables in the light of the mission of Jesus to introduce the kingdom of God. He concluded that the parables embody the essentials of the message of Jesus about the kingdom, namely, that salvation has arrived in the crisis precipitated by the coming of Jesus. Jesus offers a certainty of hope, and yet this hope comes as a challenge that men can refuse to accept. The final display of God's salvation will come only after suffering, and so, men must identify with the confident trust of Jesus in the triumph of God's plan. The believer receives the gift of salvation with joy for it enables him to have the freedom to be patient as the realization of the kingdom brings about a reversal of prevailing conditions.

Parables and the New Hermeneutic

The attractive synthesis of parable study forged by Jeremias came under attack by the existential commentators of the so-called new hermeneutic. They charged that he reduced the teaching of Jesus to a set of ideas and the parables to abstract ideas. The new hermeneutic is an attempt to return to the foundational language of the New Testament, to hear the parable as a parable-metaphor, and to bypass the derivative language, that is, the technical jargon developed by theology to translate it into dogmatic statements.

Parable language is not descriptive but performative or "assertive," that is, a "mode of language that founds a world" and grants rites of passage to it.[5] Parables are, as J. Crossan says, "the primary language of a religious experience, and as such," he adds, "they are part of the experience itself."[6] This primary language is similar to religious conversion at the deepest level. Parables, then, are not summaries of religious experience in general, but eruptions of the unique religious experience of Jesus in response to God's communicating with him and making him Messiah.

Parable language cannot be completely conceptualized, but remains open and irreducible, that is, it cannot be fully translated into any set of perfectly logical ideas. Parable is theopoetic language, a symbolic drama that creates participation in the mystery it uncovers. It is not like allegory that can be used to explain and then discarded. No; parable is never expendable; it constantly reveals anew to each one who hears. Through parable Jesus communicated his own experience of the divine presence active in and through him.

Through parable, Jesus communicates his own acceptance of the divine mystery, a reality that is grasped only in the obedience of faith. Parables offer the experience of Jesus as saving event for the hearer.

The basic principle of the new hermeneutic for understanding parables is that they interpret us, that they cast light upon who we are, where we are and where we are going, and they open to us the truth that Jesus' promises can alone make us free.[7]

Parables, then, must not be looked upon simply as instruction. Parables are revelations, revelations by Jesus of the other dimension, of the ultimate reality that God is revealing who he is in Jesus Christ — for us. Parables cannot be separated from the centrality of Jesus in God's universal plan. Parables reveal that "all life has the character of a story and of a plot, and that its denouement has come."[8] Within the overarching metaphor of eschatological fulfilment in Christ, the parable functions as an esthetical object with its own dynamism and tension, as poetic metaphor. It "essentially says what cannot be said in any other better or clearer fashion."[9]

Jesus used parables not as steps to abstract truth but as signs pointing to the kingdom, signs so related to the inbreaking of God that they opened Jesus' own path and are the means by which he invites others to join him as the Way (John 14:6) because in this way is truth and life. In other words, there is no real understanding of the parable without crying out "Abba," without embracing the kingdom; for as sign the parable has no meaning apart from the acceptance of the religious reality it reveals. To "hear" a parable is to be converted by it. A sense of parable is seen in the stories of Flannery O'Connor. What she said about her stories can offer some help to approaching parables:

> People have a habit of saying, "What is the theme of your story?" and they expect you to give them a statement: "The theme of my story is the economic

pressure of the machine on the middle class" — or some such absurdity. And when they've got a statement like that, they go off happy and feel it is no longer necessary to read the story.

One doesn't understand the parable and then make an application. No; the understanding of the parable is healing and reconciliation, because parables are paradigms of the metaphor of faith and of the world in which believers live. The acceptance of them is the commitment to the fellowship of believers and the experience of that rebirth in Christ that makes man a "new creature." How are these new insights into the power of parables being developed today?

Contemporary Parable Research

The greater appreciation of the role of parables in revealing the religious experience of Jesus has encouraged increased study of them on the part of many commentators. They are being contemplated as aesthetical objects, minidramas, artistic compositions with their own inner dynamism that reflects the power of God working in Jesus. More effort is being made to recreate the experience that the original telling created. This can be done by restoring their concreteness, "to allow them to become parables again, and that means to take them as metaphorical."[10]

As an esthetical object,[11] the parable "emerges from and returns to experience; it grows out of and reaches into the whole of life." It does not say what a person ought to do but rather discloses the horizons in which he must make his decision by bringing the everyday world into the horizon of the ultimacy of the kingdom revealed by God in Jesus.[12] When Jesus preached, he brought new vision and hope out of his own experience, for it was in the light of his experience that he saw men's lives hemmed in by selfishness and fear and ignorance and superstition and self-seeking and uncontrolled passion. He did not reject the human condition but offered compassion, freedom, and empowered vision. And in the parable form he found a way to break down man's defenses and a way to invite him to trust. To do so required a complete reversal of values, for "he who commits sin is a slave" (John 8:34). Jesus saw that sin traps man; it warps his life, clouds his vision and makes him incapable of dealing honestly with God. Unless God reaches through these defenses and breaks the hold of sin, the sinner is lost.

The parable of the spendthrift son or, better, of the father merciful toward both sons, shows God doing this (Luke 15:11-32). The young son, his resources gone, reduced to a condition of complete helplessness, decides he cannot survive without the good things his father can give him. But, in his embarrassment, he cannot claim the rights of son; he cannot look his father in the face. So he will go back as a slave for he is unable to communicate freely. But when the father sees him in this diminished state, he re-establishes communication. He refuses to deal with him as slave and restores him to sonship by his own initiative and power and gracious healing. This is the kingdom.

By linking these paradoxical situations, the parable shows the sinner where he is. The offer of grace and healing creates the moment of repentance, and language becomes saving event when the sinner accepts sonship once more and enters into the freedom that only God can give. Only when the chains of sin fall does the parable really become parable, for the "per-

son of the hearer is not outside of the process of revelation."[13]

> It is the sinner who hears, for he alone understands
> grace . . . The word of grace and the deed of grace
> divide the audience into younger sons and elder
> sons, into sinners and Pharisees. This is what Ernst
> Fuchs means when he says that one does not inter-
> pret the parables; *the parables interpret him* . . . The
> Pharisees are those who insist on interpreting the
> word of grace rather than letting themselves be inter-
> preted by it.[14]

All of the parables in some way or other draw us
into the kingdom, whether they are explicitly parables of the reign of God or not. But, within this total
context of revelation, each parable has its own insight
into the eschatological reality that Jesus is still communicating to believers. Each parable is a minidrama,
the whole good news in a dramatic scene. Each
makes available an aspect of the religious experience
of Jesus and his recognition that man is in desperate
need of God, and that man can find salvation only in
response to God's loving initiative in revelation.

Through parables Jesus communicated the trust in
the heavenly Father that he lived out in his own life
and passion and death. The great contribution of current parable study is to locate parables squarely
within the religious experience of Jesus. They are the
fruit of the vision of God and the concrete life-style
that Jesus chose as God's servant. Jesus entrusted
everything, his life, his future, the kingdom itself, to
God's concern and grace and wisdom. He celebrated
his dependence, his radical obedience.

Take, for example, the short parable in Luke 13:20-
21 (or Matthew 13:33). "What shall I compare the
reign of God to? It's something like yeast when a

woman mixes it with three measures of flour until the whole is leavened." There is a picture and a mystery, a parable, not a logical explanation. The "picture side" is the entrance into the mystery. The parable creates a new world in which the leaven is change, desacralization; the *hidden* element is mystery, inner dynamism; and the three measures (an enormous amount of flour) will point to power, to the over-whelming presence of God in the new creation. The power of God is at work in an example homey enough to use yeast, a living substance that Jews saw as impure, homey enough to speak of hiding — in the greater society in contrast to Jewish withdrawal. And yet, the example itself is shocking. Why should a woman try to knead about sixty pounds of wheat, enough to feed a village?

This short parable shows the inner dynamism as well as the unexpected possibilities of the ruling power of God. To believe this parable is to trust in the transforming power of God, even as Jesus did, and to accept the risk that this commitment involves. One who lets his life be interpreted by the word of grace communicated in this little drama accepts the king-dom as an eschatological reality and makes it the overarching metaphor of his existence. The parable has created a world for him to make good in. Funk calls this feature of parables "world-gain," that is, the enlargement of the hearer's horizons that achieves the freedom of sonship.[15]

Application to Preaching Today

These researches on the mystery of parable and their mode of offering revelation have great sig-nificance for preaching because they bring us to par-ticipate in the religious experience of Jesus. They help us see that parables cannot be fully translated into dogmatic statements. The vision of the kingdom created by the parables is grounded first of all in the life-style of Jesus and his complete openness to the Father. This vision energizes the Christian preacher. As a result, even from New Testament times, believers have used parables to illustrate moral lessons.

Some of these applications are found already in the New Testament itself. The exciting parable of the incompetent manager in Luke 16:1-7, for example, has attached to it four different applications. The parable itself, which ends at verse 7, is the story of a hired manager who has just been reported to the owner as not making a profit from his land. This parable begins in crisis, and its dramatic movement goes from crisis to response to denouement. Faced with the crisis of being cut off from his livelihood, the manager is shocked into action. For the first time, he sees that life is not his private possession to control or manipulate, that he must receive it as a gift. And so he quickly arranges with the owner's debtors to substitute smaller IOU's for the debts they owe. And that is the parable. How am I living life? Do I live out this single moment of eschatological crisis as a gift, or have I been relying on myself to make good out of life?

Such a striking parable would obviously invite application. It must also have struck some early believers as needing a conclusion. And so the first attached application begins by specifying, "The Lord (Jesus) praised the manager who could not justify his own life in that he had reacted prudently," and it then makes a comparison between religious and worldly persons. Then Luke adds a warning on the correct use of wealth (verse 9). The third addition is on trustworthiness, and may be related to the parable of

the ten coins in Luke 19:11-27. The fourth addition
deals with the fundamental option of life that the
kingdom demands. These additions show that the
primitive Christian community was already applying
parables to various challenges arising in living out the
Christian life. It is legitimate, then, to draw moral
lessons from the parables, but it would be a distortion
to limit them to moral instruction.

The nature of a parable is to be open-ended; they
are not complete either in hearing or preaching until
the hearer is drawn into the response they create.
Parables remain a part of Christian preaching as they
confront the believers of each generation to embrace
the mystery of the kingdom. This kingdom is not
simply God's new availability in Jesus Christ, but also
the grace of man's transformed existence created by
the revelation of Christ and the gift of his Spirit. The
parables reveal this new situation of man in a variety
of ways, and as such they are a school of humility.

Parables also make us Eucharistic, a thank-you
people. If we look, for example, at the parable of the
good Samaritan, we see Jesus confronting his audience with a crisis. A man has fallen among thieves
and lies in the ditch. What happens? The man is ignored by the priest and by the levite. Immediately,
the hearers identify with the man in the ditch: life is
one big ditch, and all the do-gooders in the world
don't change things. But no! there is hope! Someone
does stop. And then, greater despair for the victim.
Help comes from the hated Samaritan. An unexpected denouement.

The parable has placed the hearers under judgment. Will they accept salvation as a free and unexpected gift? Will they respond to the possibility of an

existence under God's universal saving power and place no limits upon the gift? The heavenly Father *is* compassion (Luke 6:36), his love is universal. This parable, then, reveals where the hearer is. It interprets the lie of the sinner who wants to put conditions upon God's saving grace. To hear is to accept the reality of universal brotherhood, to say "sin stops here" (Luke 10:30-37). Parables shatter the prison of sin, selfishness and fear.

Part of the impact of the parable is the shock it creates as instrumental in a recognition of reality. This is why some of the parables begin with the question, "To what will I compare the kingdom of heaven," which simply means, "Would you believe it if I told you that the kingdom of heaven was able to be compared to. . . ?" It is a mystery too good to be believed.

With the help of contemporary parable research, the preaching of parables can be a fruitful source of didascalia, of Christian contemplation. By enabling his hearers to hear the parables once again as parables, instead of as moral instructions or allegories, the preacher can open to them the reversal that Christ's coming implies so that they may find liberating communion with the Trinity. Parables reveal how "the kingdom arrives and breaks in upon a man so that he experiences God's rule at the moment when his own world is turned upside down and radically reversed."[16]

Parables say in poetic image that there is no other name under heaven whereby man is saved except in Jesus, in sharing his kenosis and exaltation. They are so much a part of Christian revelation that they cannot be superseded. They were the form of revelation exploited by Jesus to bring his hearers to their fundamental responsibility in life, that is, to recognize and respond to God's saving grace.

Understanding a parable comes from entering into its plot.[17] Each particular parable-plot enables us to enter the total divine "plot" or plan of salvation. Unless our preaching of parables brings believers to reaffirm their basic faith decision, that preaching is a betrayal of the parables and of the kingdom. To preach the parable as parable requires that the preacher is living in the world created by the revelation of Jesus, the world in which God's grace interprets his life. Perhaps the famous dictum of Bengal applies nowhere so well as to the study of the parables, "Apply yourself totally to the text; apply the text totally to yourself."

8.
Trinitarian Experience in the Word

The parables about the reign of God flow from the desire of Jesus to point out the universal care of his Father for men. It is this reality that Jesus saw so clearly that has prompted Christians to create a "theology," which in its radical sense means "God becoming language." This theology is an attempt to conceptualize how God makes himself available to men in human communication.

We have seen in the preceding chapter how the parables interpret human existence for man, how they assure us that God's love creates the world in which men can find their individual and communal happiness. The parables communicate the God-experience of Jesus, his vision of the saving power of God's love, and his awareness that his existence was the offer to men of divine grace experienced in man's liberation and unending happiness. Human destiny is not some *thing* but the ability to share in the experience of God that Jesus enjoys, an experience that shattered and re-created history, an experience that brings all divine promises to fulfillment (see Acts 13:33).

What Jesus experienced was a creative freedom, boundless self-giving, reconciling power, a community of happiness in complete personal sharing. What the writers of the Gospels did was to communicate to men, who did not have the opportunity to see the earthly Jesus, the impact of his presence upon the primitive community so that all men might have a chance to celebrate the experience of God enjoyed by Jesus. Here, we want to try to enter into this celebration of the Trinitarian experience by Jesus, to let some of the experiences of the life of Jesus bring God into our language so that he may share himself with us. We shall consider, first, his baptism, transfiguration, and passion, seeing in these events how the self-consciousness of Jesus as Son of God surfaces. We shall then see how the words of Jesus invite us to experience the Father. Finally, we shall examine how Jesus related to the Holy Spirit.

Events Witnessing to Jesus' Identity

What happened to Jesus at his baptism is important because in it he experienced some special sign of divine approval. Whether this experience was externalized or not, and how he shared it with others is still being discussed by exegetes. In any case, Jesus did receive into his consciousness a vivid divine affirmation of his sonship and mission.

But for our celebration of the experience of Jesus, it is perhaps more important to ask why Jesus decided to be baptized at all. His decision to undergo this rite of repentance and conversion show us how he envisioned the mission entrusted to him by his Father. He had the conviction that God wanted him to identify with sinful mankind, with human helplessness and alienation. He felt that he was not to keep aloof from human needs and longings. In him God was reconciling men not from afar, not from the highest heaven, but from within the human condition. Jesus was the expression of God's saving compassion.

In undergoing baptism, then, Jesus celebrated humble-mindedness and repentance, confidence in God's care and hope in reconciliation as actions by which God opens up to men the experience of his presence. By trust in God we live and move and become fully alive because human destiny is to accept liberation as a gift from God. "Be compassionate as your heavenly Father is compassionate" (Luke 6:36).

In his transfiguration there was another bursting of the divine into the consciousness of Jesus. The event is connected with the turning point in his public life. Jesus had reached the point when he saw that the majority were not going to open themselves to his vision of God. He would not be accepted by his own people. Since he could not cease bearing witness to his Father's love, he knew that he would have to face death to show that God is really man's only destiny. It was because of this realization that Jesus devoted more time now to instructing his chosen disciples, preparing them for his rejection by his own people.

But with this knowledge of impending rejection, Jesus knew another experience: an ineffable moment of transfiguration. It was a God-experience so intense that it became visible in his body. And once more the Father assured Jesus that he was the beloved Son whose life was to transform human destiny.

This unique God-consciousness surfaces once more during the trial scene when the high priest asks Jesus if he claims the title of Son of God. Jesus not only accepts this title but specifies it by claiming to be Son of God in a unique way, not simply as chosen king but as the heavenly Son of Man of the apocalyptic writings. He is Son, not in the general way of the Jewish king as anointed, but in the very origin of his being. In fact, being Son defines his whole existence.

To be able to share and communicate and celebrate with his heavenly Father is what gives him life and makes him life for men. Jesus embraces death in the sense that this act of perfect submission is destined to open men up to God in a way that no words or miracles could do. His perfect trust draws all men into the loving community he enjoys with the Father. But what is this community of life?

Jesus' Offer of the Experience of the Father

The entire earthly life of Jesus was a revelation, an uncovering of the reality of God in the sense that he spoke and acted in a way that enabled men to experience God's availability to them. Of course, men, and in a special way, the Jews, had experienced God. But Jesus presented his life-style as fulfilling the promise of the prophets of a new age, an age of joyful and unending intimacy with God. God would no longer limit his sharing to a covenant that had to be written and studied and renewed. No; he would become available in an undreamed of way. As Paul put it: "God was in Jesus Christ reconciling the world to himself" (2 Cor. 5:19). God makes himself present to men in and through Jesus as a reconciling presence, a liberating presence, a consoling presence, a supporting and encouraging presence, a presence that creates; in a word, God is personally present as an actor, a subject, in our lives.

Jesus then was to be "good news," God's promise of friendship. What Jesus was conscious of was that God was doing this in him, through the actual experience that he enjoyed on this earth. The nature of this experience appears in the way that Jesus speaks of "the Father" or of "my Father" when talking to others. He does not say "our Father." It is only when he has completed his earthly experience and has let men see God's presence at work that he will tell men to pray together, "our Father." With his coming no man can remain aloof from the common destiny of all mankind. His Father is above all things else Savior, the all-embracing Thou, not only of each individual, but of the entire human race. To accept God as Father is to live out the total *Yes* in Christ, as Paul says clearly (2 Cor. 1:19).

The experience of the Father by Christ was that God accepted all who received him (Matthew 10:32-33), that man had to open himself to the Father's plan to enter into his reign (Matthew 7:21). Jesus experienced that a total Yes to the Father was the condition of experiencing the wisdom and friendship and power and freedom of God. Man can celebrate life on its deepest level only by entering into that mutual sharing that Jesus experienced with his Father. It is an ongoing, mutual, intensely personal communion.

But how can men pronounce that Yes, which is so demanding and so full of risk? The purpose of the Word becoming man was simply to reveal how. All the words and deeds of Jesus had no other purpose than to offer man light and strength to do this. Above all, his great act of love on Calvary — "the school of love" — where he offered his own life as "ransom" (Mark 10:45). Perhaps all of this can be best summarized by looking at the famous "Johannine" saying found in Matthew 11:25-30.

> At that time Jesus exclaimed, "I bless you, Father, Lord of heaven and of earth, for hiding these things from the learned and the clever and revealing them to mere children. Yes, Father, for that is what it pleased you to do. Everything has been entrusted to me by my Father; and no one knows the Father except the Son and those to whom the Son chooses to reveal him.

> Come to me, all you who labor and are overbur-
> dened, and I will give you rest. Shoulder my yoke
> and learn from me, for I am gentle and humble in
> heart, and you will find rest for your souls. Yes, my
> yoke is easy and my burden light.

Matthew 11:25-27 is an exclamation of praise and
thanks, celebrating the Father for making himself
available to the "little ones" by handing all things
over into their hands. This saying calls to mind the
final words of Matthew's Gospel when the risen Jesus
gathers his disciples together and invites them to
share the fulness of his Father's power, and to offer
the experience of it to all men (see Matthew 28:16-20).
The link between these two scenes shows that the
"little ones" are not a special class, but rather all men
in their relationship to God as Father. Men can experience the Father only by becoming a child, a son in
the Son, adopting his obedient humble-mindedness.

Matthew 11:28-30 expresses the corresponding side
of the experience of the Father. Here Jesus presents
himself in the person of divine Wisdom inviting all of
these little ones to come to him and be refreshed.
Man can enjoy the experience of God only when he
learns the life-style of Jesus, a life lived always in and
for the Father. From his own inner joy and peace,
Jesus knows that only God's life shared with men can
satisfy the human spirit and thus proclaim the great
truth of Scripture of the primacy of the spiritual. But
this brings us to consider the experience of the Holy
Spirit by Jesus.

The Experience of the Holy Spirit and Jesus

Actually, the gospels do not describe at any great
length the role of the Holy Spirit in the God-

experience of Jesus. On the one hand, the Holy Spirit seems to be superior to Jesus because his whole life is lived under the guidance of the Spirit. He was born by the power of the Holy Spirit; he drove out devils by the Spirit. The personality of the Holy Spirit is not clearly presented, and at times his activity seems to be simply the reconciling power of God at work.

And yet, Jesus promises to send the Holy Spirit upon his disciples. This paradoxical relationship surpasses the laws of human logic and creates a new dimension of the God-experience that became clear only in the actual experience of the apostolic Church. Christians were swept up into that exciting, ongoing interchange that was taking place between Jesus and his Spirit.

And, in the final analysis, this is what the life of Jesus says to us. To know God as person, to experience him as our All, is not an abstraction but a celebration, a loving, surrendering interchange. The life that Jesus led on earth was possible only because he was willing to let God maintain the initiative, willing to be led by the Spirit whether this led to the desert or to death on Calvary, willing to trust his whole life to the Father's hands. The actual external manifestation of this surrender will take many forms, and will vary in the life of each individual and community as circumstances change. But this is the call and challenge of Jesus now.

Paul's Trinitarian Experience

How can we describe this challenge of Trinitarian life in the early Church? How can we describe it, for instance, in Paul? What was the challenge to Paul of whom Chrysostom said, "The heart of Paul is the heart of Christ"? It is interesting that Paul insists strongly that he is a monotheist; he believes in only one God (see Rom. 1:25). Paul's God is the father of the Lord Jesus Christ. He is unique creator and savior of all men. In Paul, as well as in other New Testament writers, where the word God appears with the article, the author is speaking of the Father.[1]

Paul calls Christ God only once, in the prayerful exclamation of Romans 9:5, where he bursts forth in the doxology to celebrate Christ as "blessed God forever. Amen." How then did Jesus fit into his God-experience? Not as a rival nor as a second God, but as God-with-us, as God's visible availability, as the sign of God's care and the promise of God's saving power. Paul never tried to resolve the tension between his strict monotheism and the centrality of Christ in human history. On the contrary, the disclosure of this tension is what opened Paul's life to the unbelievably rich new appreciation of the one true God whom he had worshiped as a Jew. And so he invites men to proclaim, "Jesus is Lord, to the glory of God the Father" (Phil. 2:11).

Christ is mirror of the Father; in him the Father has envisioned and created all things; through him all creation will return to the Father (see 1 Cor 15:24-28; Col 1:16). In the carrying out of God's plan there is certainly a functional subordination of Christ to the Father, but this subordination is so complete and harmonious that it can be accomplished only by the Son who is the perfect model of the Father, working in an exciting unity with him, and therefore, in human terms, equal to the Father. It would take Christian theologians over three hundred years to formulate this experience in technical concepts. But we would be unfaithful to the goal of the great Christological formulas if we did not use them to enter more fully into the experience of God that Paul enjoyed.

In making his profession of faith, the new believer pledged himself to pursue the possibilities of the Lordship of Jesus, to embrace the challenge of living *in Christ*, to accept the risen Lord Jesus as the very air that sustained his spirit, the ground that supported his freedom, the power that gave him courage to grow, the light to search for truth, the presence that promised joy and reconciliation. A profession of faith in Jesus Christ is a challenge to live a new dimension of life, a call to identify with the mind-set of Jesus crucified and glorified, and the call to join hands with all of those who wish to build an unselfish community of love in and through life.

It is clear from Paul's letters that he conceived of the individual communities as assemblies of worship, as groups impelled by a life of common prayer. He always ends his opening salutation with a "blessing," a prayer invoking God's "grace and peace," that is, his healing presence and saving help upon the community. With regard to Paul's God-experience, the striking part about his blessings is that they mention only the Father and the Lord Jesus Christ, seldom the Holy Spirit.

What, then, about the Holy Spirit? Didn't Paul pray to him? Actually, only on one occasion in his letters does Paul pronounce what we would call a Trinitarian blessing upon the community. This is at the end of the Second Letter to the Corinthians and is used as one of the three blessings of the new liturgy: "The grace of the Lord Jesus Christ and the agape-love of God and the fellowship of the Holy Spirit be with all of you" (2 Cor. 13:13). It marks a fitting close to the correspondence with the community that had experienced so visibly the active presence of the Holy Spirit through his extraordinary charisms. But is this one prayer enough to call Paul's faith Trinitarian? Did Paul really experience the Holy Spirit as divine?

If we would limit our consideration of the God-experience of Paul to explicit professions of faith and prayers, we could conclude that Paul communed on a personal level only with the Father and Jesus as transcendent Thou's. And yet, when we enter into the rhythm of his letters as a whole, a remarkable Trinitarian pattern emerges. The full scope of the penetration of the Holy Spirit into molding the heart of Paul appears only when he undertakes to offer to his readers a guide for their personal, daily life-style.

Then it becomes clear that his own life was the result of an effective cooperation and exchange within his inner space of the love that the Father, Son, and Holy Spirit are exercising among themselves and toward men. Paul experienced the Father in the reality and majesty of creation and re-creation; he knew the wisdom of the Son in the folly of the Cross; but he also experienced the continual, invisible, sustaining presence of the Holy Spirit prompting him to a life of unselfishness and sacrifice even to death in union with the self-giving of Jesus.

A Trinitarian Life-style

Like Paul, all men must reach out for courage to celebrate the gifts he recognizes in himself as valuable and yet so fragile. Man needs the courage to risk, Jesus said, for "he who loves his life loses it." Only in the risk of loss is life found. By his own life-style Jesus showed his disciples that to risk the trust in his Father's love and care was real living. And he invited men to come to him because it was by becoming involved in his experience of God that we take the ultimate risk of life.

It is this risk of life in Jesus that is the condition of developing a Trinitarian life-style. This risk is the condition for developing the Christian framework, the overarching attitude toward life we see in the apostles. We accept the common responsibility to build up community in love, but we accept this responsibility as a gift of the Spirit blossoming forth in joy, peace, patience, graciousness, goodness, loyalty, self-control (Gal. 5:22-23).

The scene in Acts 19, where the disciples of John the Baptist receive the Holy Spirit, illustrates that the receiving of the gift of his indwelling is essential for enjoying the Trinitarian experience. With God's new availability to men in Jesus, there is a new creation, and this new situation demands an appropriate life-style. But this life-style itself is a gift, not a human creation. The willingness to accept life as a gift is the necessary condition for celebrating Christian existence. This openness brings us the liberating power to rejoice in and boast about our own weakness as an expression of God's saving dynamism. God prepared man for this life-style by creating him in his image. The life of Jesus in his perfect openness to his Father is the perfection of this new life-style, which finds its purest form of celebration on Calvary.

In Christ's life and death we experience the availability of God's presence among men. His self-emptying, self-renouncement even to the surrender of his life was openness and the risk of trust. Hence, it is a continual quality of the Trinitarian existence. Our life is hidden with Christ in God, accepting the plan and care of God for us. This is what Paul mys-

teriously calls "the faith of Christ." [1a] And the heart of
Paul's letter to the Romans, those great chapters five
through eight, describe the life of Christ, life in his
Spirit, as the life enjoyed by those who accept the risk
of faith.

The crucial role of faith is that it lets God be God.
Faith opens up to God as initiator of salvation. Once
present, God sets up the condition for a Christian
life-style by generating the trinity of faith, hope and
love. Paul sees Christian life-style as the unfolding of
these gifts in attitude, action, and communication. It
is important to recognize these gifts as the source of
real living, especially in this period when the good in
all forms of religious experience is being recognized.

The point is this: it is not arrogance to insist upon
the uniqueness of Christ as God's Good News and to
attribute all saving activity to the gift of his Spirit.
This is not to deny the presence of Christ and his
Spirit in all human conditions. It is simply to say that
no man is his own savior. Faith is the universal quality that prevents men from becoming self-satisfied
and so of cutting themselves off from the dynamism
of God's saving presence in their lives. Faith prevents
religious experience from becoming pure phantasy,
pure subjectivism.

By showing men their own limitations, faith enables them to accept their personal and corporate responsibility for faith unfolds the reality of a divine
plan carried out by free saving activity on God's part
in the world and in a unique way in Jesus Christ, a
plan operative in individual lives by the power of the
Spirit of Christ. Faith also assures individuals as persons and as social beings that God is leading them to
a transcendent destiny and to common reconciliation
in Sonship.

Faith, in other words, is the call to experience mystery, to enter into the highest possibilities of human experience. When a person enters upon this experience, he wants to celebrate it in all possible ways: intellectually, by reflecting on it and describing it and articulating it in a systematic way; socially, by sharing it with others and receiving support from their experience. The mystery that faith celebrates is the reality of God becoming man's destiny and fulfilment and reconciliation. God's availability to man in this personal way is the ultimate in giving. It was this experience that made John exclaim, "God is love" (1 John 4:8,16). Man can still reject this offer, but when he freely accepts, he opens his spirit to hope and love as the celebration his spirit strives for.

Historically, the self-giving of God reached its unique expression in the Incarnation understood in its overarching sweep from virginal conception through the glorification of Jesus in his return to the Father as Savior and final judge of living and dead. This historical availability continues to be offered to believers in the Holy Spirit. This continuing availability of God enables man to maintain the primacy of the spiritual without sacrificing the reality of his historical situation. He receives the means of integrating the profane, the prosaic, the trite, the material, the nitty-gritty of his daily existence into the new creation in Christ, the key, the ground, the raison d'etre, the crown of God's presence and power, to whom he opens himself.

The believer celebrates Christ as liberating gift and final healing. As liberating gift, Christ is celebrated in contemplation, in sacramental encounter, in community sharing, in creative service of mankind. As final healing, he is "hope of the world, God of all compassion." Trinitarian life-style simply manifests this faith, hope, and love in everyday living. God as Father, Son, and Holy Spirit becomes the interpreter of all experience so that man can reach the point where it is possible to say with Paul, "I live, now no longer I, but Christ lives in me" (Gal. 2:20). This is living "in faith."

This inbreaking of God as the Father of our Lord Jesus Christ turned Paul's life upside down. It made him reject all that he had counted on before for support and security. In his letter to the Philippians (3:7-9), Paul gives us a personal articulation of his Christian experience:

> Whatever things were to my advantage, on Christ's account I consider these a hindrance . . . More than that, I even consider everything to be a hindrance on account of the overarching power of knowing Christ Jesus my Lord. On his account I have written everything off as loss, and I consider everything as so much rubbish so that I may have the advantage of sharing Christ. Let God find me in him, not being acceptable because of what I am myself but because of faith in Christ, that is, being acceptable to God in virtue of faith.

Paul here speaks of his lived experience, the new world that opened up to him when God called him to be witness to his love in Jesus Christ. This call led to a change in Paul's value system. His judgments and his life-style were no longer controlled by the external norm of Mosaic observance. No; God accepted him as friend because he took the risk of trusting himself to the Lord Jesus. For the believer, no value, no activity of personal or communal living can remain outside of the all-embracing reality of God's life shared in Jesus Christ.

The born Christian might say that this experience of Paul does not really apply. Yet there was growth in

Paul. The Christ-experience is active, continually transforming. A believer is devoted to life. No doubt this is why Paul adds the attitudes of hope or endurance and agape-love to faith as the triad that summarizes the Trinitarian experience in life-style. For these three create "a greeting, an embrace, a welcome,"[2] that is, they set up a spirit of receptivity toward God in all of his comings; a spirit of celebrating the conditions of life which can be seen in his total providence, and a spirit of going out in self-giving to welcome others into the joy of being accepted by God. The Church then becomes the community of those coming together to give themselves and God to one another and to all mankind.

A Trinitarian life-style has no need for anxiety. It is the opponent of all self-seeking. It alone can bring men to the goal of all creation, the praise of God. The opening blessing of Ephesians 1:3-14 is really a celebration of the Trinitarian experience. Through openness to the activity of the Father, Son, and Holy Spirit by the life-style of faith, hope and love, the Christian community becomes the temple Body of Christ that reconciles the world to the Father. This is the one celebration worth living.

The Apostolic Community as a Trinitarian Experience

The Trinitarian experience of the early community was often a stormy voyage. It did not produce a monolithic society. On the contrary, what is always striking about the New Testament community is the variety of ways which the inbreaking of God in Jesus Christ evoked response personally and as a group, ways that continually adapted to changing situations and that attracted an ever-increasing number of believers and spread rapidly among different peoples.

Grounding this variety of Church organizations and life-styles was the profound loyalty to the Father of the Lord Jesus and a sense of oneness in his ever-present Spirit. Often a simple incident or even a single sentence opens up creative insights into how this experience permeated the lives of the primitive members and how it can transform men today.

This is why the Christian community in its search for renewal must always return to the New Testament experience to authenticate its celebration of Christian freedom in new situations, and especially in a climate where, "because of our rapidly evolving understanding of man, the world, and the Church,"[3] we need a more flexible and creative response to the gifts God has given us in Jesus Christ. In a talk on "Wider Horizons,"[4] Thomas Berry related to this need when he spoke about the inability of formalized religion to speak to college students today. He said that among them "there is such a closed-off view of western real spiritual tradition; because there is so much general cynicism, they are kind of hardened to it, stiffened to it, and they cannot experience it."

In an age when national morale is low, this blanket of cynicism and discouragement tends to engulf everyone and every effort. It is a form of indifference which psychologists tell us is the real opposition to love. What then can we do to revive among ourselves both as individuals and as a community this Trinitarian experience?

In its best sense, renewal means letting the authentic experience of the apostolic Church shape the adaptation of our particular tradition in its role of shaping history now. It needs groupings of religious people who have freely chosen to give their lives and talents and hopes into the hands of the Lord Jesus for the building up of the reign of God. If man is celebrant of life, how much more so the dedicated Christian. Religious must mobilize their gifts to celebrate the Trinitarian experience.

Before looking at how the New Testament community became celebrants of Father, Son, and Holy Spirit, it is necessary to say a word about experience. Why this stress? Because experience is man's special prerogative; it is his involvement as a free being. At the same time, man is infinitely complex. He has all kinds of avenues of possibilities open, and an infinite variety of motivation even for the same mode of action. Today the behavioral sciences are giving us a better appreciation of the unchartered frontiers of man's inner space. They are working to analyze these areas. In particular, the human growth potential movement is investigating possibilities and methods of human growth that men will be better able to celebrate life and live in enriching community of life.

If we tried to express the most profound depths of man, what regulates his stance toward life, we would have to agree with Karl Rahner[5] that it is freedom — freedom in the active sense of the possibility and responsibility to transcend self, to respond to the transcendent mystery that is God. Man remains and becomes fully man only when he exercises his capacity for the infinite. His life then is guided by this experience of God, a celebration so unique that no one can exchange it or communicate it fully.

In the most general terms humans have three media to experience reality, namely, their senses, their intellectual powers, and, for want of a better word, their spiritual capacity, which is closely linked to their will. No matter what avenue they use, it is always the whole person who experiences. Through

1124 *Preaching* GOD'S BURNING WORD

the senses man comes into contact with material creation; through his intellectual powers he opens his
being to shared understanding; and through his spirit
he enjoys prayerful or mystical experience.

The point of all this is that the Trinitarian dimension
of one's religious life-style is developed on all levels of
experience. The Trinitarian mystery beckons to us for,
as Karl Rahner points out, the Trinity is the ultimate
mystery.[6] God is available to us through his enflesh-
ment in Jesus Christ and his presence in the Holy
Spirit. The New Testament community shows us the
possibility of celebrating this mystery in creative love
and joyful obedience.

When we let the New Testament speak, we find
that we come into a community that is alive and
happy. Their happiness was not the result of naivete
or of isolation from reality. They were aware of press-
ing social problems, of all forms of pressures and
prejudices against them. But they were able to endure
and thrive and grow because they had a constructive
attitude toward life and toward all the crucial decisions that make life a celebration.

The community's experience was a response to the
reality of God presenting himself in a more universal
and transforming way. Historically, Christianity has
tended to emphasize the intellectual aspect of God's
self-giving — to formulate creeds. But with the return
of the global village, religious thinkers are placing
more emphasis on other dimensions of the Christian
experience.[7] Indeed, religious experience itself,
which enables a person to integrate the holy and the
profane, calls for a fuller celebration of life. What we
must note here is that "the crises of human life are
disclosures of the holy only when authenticated by a
public disclosure of revelation," that "revelation is

the necessary fuller development of religious experience."

If, then, we can break through that language barrier that tends to dull our response, and if we can find a way of identifying more fully with the experience of God in Jesus that Peter and the other disciples had, then our faith should be a real source of light and peace for us, for it will be a celebration of that exciting "self-communication possession"[8] that is Father, Son, and Holy Spirit.

Appropriating the Trinitarian Experience

The New Testament community experience was really a process of interiorizing the Christ-event. This found expression chiefly at community liturgical celebrations. These were, and still are, the pinnacle of Christian experience, the characteristic mark of the followers of Jesus. "Do this in my memory." The community liturgical assembly is not an escape from reality. It is a celebration of God's presence in Jesus, who continues his saving activity in his Holy Spirit. Here believers receive instruction and inner power; they share God with one another and offer mutual support and insight. By growing in their understanding of what the lordship of Jesus means in their own lives and in their service of the world, the community becomes the living Body of Christ for mankind.

Acts of the Apostles indicate that the apostolic community asked new members simply to acknowledge the lordship of Jesus. This was the first profession of Christian faith. The new believer would simply acknowledge a unique presence of God in Jesus Christ. He would celebrate his faith by the creedal statement, "I believe unto the Lord Jesus," or "I believe that Jesus is Lord." Simple as this statement sounds, it was really a revolutionary view of God, for it proclaimed that the God of history and of the Jewish people, who had revealed himself to Moses, was now vitally present in a unique and effective way in the world in the risen Jesus.

Jesus Christ, then, did not tell something about God; he is a new presence of God to men and for men, a presence that reveals God as the Father who gives his Son for men and receives an obedience of perfect surrender, even unto death. Before this time God had revealed himself in acts of power and loving kindness and compassion. Now he reveals a new dimension of his being, his redemptive love in the total self-giving of his Son. This death is the fulness of God's self-revelation. The primitive community did not expect God to tell them anything more about himself than he had said in the death and resurrection of Jesus.

In proclaiming "Jesus is Lord," the community was entering into a drama that could not leave men untouched. They were being drawn into a community of interacting beings whose very existence was an interrelatedness in knowledge and love. By entering the human situation and making himself available as redeemer in self-surrender, the divine Son was making it possible for men to share the divine community of love. Human existence received new direction and dimension, and so the life of every existing human becomes interrelated. By being established in Christ, believers are destined to build up human community into a oneness in Christ. As Lord of all, Jesus calls all men to new dignity, and he gives to his followers the duty and privilege of building up the human community in love and dignity.

In making known his glory to them in the Lord

Jesus, God was making his own life and power available, because when God reveals, it is to offer himself. His revelation creates theo-logy, which, in its deepest sense is God-becoming-language. It takes time to respond, and the time spent in doing so is called prayer and, more specifically, contemplation. "Celebrate the Lord Jesus in your hearts," says Paul. In him, God reveals what it is to be God, especially in the redemptive death, which is the great act of love. And this is what love is: giving all.

To conclude, the centrality of Jesus Christ eventually forces the fuller development of Trinitarian theology: his relation to the Father and his gift of the Spirit. Baptism provided the occasion for homilies about this experience. Actually, however, the New Testament has preserved only one Trinitarian baptismal formula. This comes at an important place, as the climax of Matthew's gospel, the Church Gospel. Matthew has built up his gospel in such a way that every action of Jesus is a step in founding the community: providing its moral guidance, its leaders, explaining its nature in parable. Finally, after his Resurrection, Jesus assembles the leaders of his Church and gives them the instruction that will guide them in forming the Church. What Matthew wishes to communicate to future generations is the lived experience of the community. This final scene, then, consists of three elements:

1. *a revelation:* God has made Jesus lord, eschatological judge of all mankind. To carry out this role, Jesus is communicating this power to his disciples.

2. *a command:* to exercise the fulness of power for the salvation of men, teaching the Good News of God and his saving will, initiating men into the Trinitarian experience through baptism.

3. *a promise:* to be with his community to enable them to carry out this command by his efficacious power and supreme authority.

The Trinitarian experience for the community is the experience of God's saving power in Jesus Christ. This means that God initiates and fosters a transforming fellowship in Jesus Christ to rescue men from alienation, from a lack of hope and purpose and peace in their existence. It means that God's presence is available in the continuing saving activity of the community, that this is not an abstract, intellectual presence, but the creativity of divine love always renewing men. It means, finally, that this presence of God in Jesus Christ and his Spirit places men under judgment: to avoid arrogance in dealing with their fellowmen and to seek reconciliation first with God, then with one another.

NOTES TO CHAPTER ONE, pages 7–22

[1] Pope Paul VI, *Address on Exegesis and Hermeneutics to the XXI Italian Biblical Week*, September 25, 1970; translated in the English edition of *L'Osservatore Romano* of October 8, 1970.

[2] Louis Dupré, *The Other Dimension: A Search for the Meaning of Religious Attitudes* (Garden City: Doubleday, 1972) p. 42.

[3] See recent books devoted to religious language, e.g., Langdon B. Gilkey, *Naming the Whirlwind: The Renewal of God-Language* (Indianapolis: Bobbs-Merrill, 1969); Paul Van Buren, *The Edges of Language: An Essay in the Logic of Religion* (London: S.C.M. Press, 1972). The current interest in the linguistic theories of the English philosopher, J. L. Austin, has had an impact on religious language also.

[4] See Bernard Lonergan, *Method in Theology* (New York: Herder and Herder, 1972).

[5] The Catholic Biblical Association letter of September 14, 1973, appears in the *Catholic Biblical Quarterly* 35 (1973) 502–506.

[6] Amos N. Wilder, "Theology and Theopoetic," *Christian Century*, May 23, 1973, p. 593.

[7] Theodore Weeden posed the question, "Is the Resurrection an Offense to Faith?" as the lead article for the Easter, 1972, issue of the *Christian Century*. He used this article to point out contemporary opposition to resurrection imagery.

[8] See Amos N. Wilder, *Early Christian Rhetoric: The Language of the Gospel* (Cambridge: Harvard University Press, 1971) for the significance of the new speech-forms created by the primitive Christian communities. "Behind the particular New Testament forms lies a particular life-experience and a language-shaping faith" (p. 9).

[9] See Eugene A. Nida, and C. R. Taber, *The Theory and Practice of Translation* (Leiden: E. J. Brill, 1969) for a developed treatment of this approach.

NOTES TO CHAPTER TWO, pages 23–36

[1] James M. Reese, "Preaching the Burning Word," *The BIBLE Today* 68 (November 1973) 1296.

[2] J. Lindblom, *Prophecy in Ancient Israel* (Philadelphia: Fortress Press, 1962) pp. 1–2.

[3] The significance of religious language will be treated at length in chapter 4. The relevance of the subject can be seen in the choice of the title for volume 85 of the new *Concilium* series, edited by J. B. Metz and J.-P. Jossua, *The Crisis of Religious Language* (New York: Herder and Herder, 1973).

[4] Leslie Dewart, *Religion, Language and Truth* (New York: Herder and Herder, 1970) p. 18, with an elaboration on pp. 29–62.

[5] An extremely helpful study for developing this awareness is Ronald Goldman, *Religious Thinking from Childhood to Adolescence* (New York: Seabury, 1968).

[6] James M. Reese, *The BIBLE Today* 68 (November 1973) p. 1298.

[7] J. Lindblom, *Prophecy*, p. 192.

[8] Amos N. Wilder, "Theology and Theopoetic," *The Christian Century* 90 (May 23, 1973) pp. 593–596. The first use of the term "theopoetic" in print that I have found is in the preface to his collection of poems, *Grace Confounding* (Philadelphia: Fortress Press, 1972), although in private conversation Wilder directed me to the use of *theo-poiesis* by S. R. Hopper in his introduction to *Interpretation: The Poetry of Meaning* (New York, Harcourt, Brace & World, 1967).

[9] The image comes from St. Ambrose according to M. Jourjon, "Rompre le pain de la parole," in *L'Homme devant Dieu: Mélanges offerts au Pere Henri de Lubac* (Paris: Aubier, 1963) 1.321–325.

[10] Henri de Lubac, *Exégèse mediévale: Les quatre sens de l'Ecriture* (Paris: Aubier, 1964) I. 323.

[11] Amos N. Wilder, "Theology and Theopoetic," p. 596.

[12] Bernard Lonergan, *Method in Theology* (New York: Herder and Herder, 1972).

NOTES TO CHAPTER THREE, *pages 37–48*

[1] Louis Dupré, *The Other Dimension: A Search for the Meaning of Religious Attitudes* (Garden City: Doubleday, 1972) p. 202.

[2] Eugene A. Nida, "Implications of Contemporary Linguistics for Biblical Scholarship," *Journal of Biblical Literature* 91 (1972) pp. 73–89.

[3] Lest preachers think that these exercises are too esoteric, they will find transformational grammar dealt with in a manual prepared for elementary school teachers, namely, G. G. Duffy, *Teaching Linguistics* (Dansville, New York: Instructor Publications, 1969) p. 25. I have provided some examples in the appendage to Chapter I.

[4] E. A. Nida and C. R. Taber, *The Theory and Practice of Translation* (Leiden: E. J. Brill, 1969) p. 98.

[5] For a development of the implications of the role of the text in calling forth response, see Paul Ricoeur, "Philosophy and Religious Language," *Journal of Religion* 54 (1974) 71–85.

[6] Irenaeus, *Adversus haereses* 4.20; at times, only the first half of the sentence is quoted, and the implication is lost.

NOTES TO CHAPTER FOUR, *pages 49–59*

[1] See note 7 of chapter I.

[2] *Summa Theologica* I, 13, 5–7.

[3] Joseph A. Fitzmyer, "The Languages of Palestine in the First Century A. D.," *Catholic Biblical Quarterly* 32 (1970) 501–531. See Jose O'Callaghan, "Papiros neotestamentarios en la cueva 7 de Qumran?" *Biblica* 53 (1972) 91–100. This is an argument for seeing a small Greek fragment in Cave 7 of Qumran which dates from about 50 A.D. as part of Mark's Gospel. However, the fragment is too minute (only 19 letters) to warrant firm conclusions,

and most scholars who studied the document have rejected his interpretation.

⁴ Morton Smith claims that the Greek fragment of a secret gospel which he discovered at the monastery of Mar Saba in the Judean desert in 1958 is earlier than the canonical Gospel of Mark. He gives an exciting account of his discovery in the popular shocker entitled *The Secret Gospel* (New York: Harper and Row, 1973). If his find could be verified, it would point to a very early use of Greek as a vehicle for writing by the Christian community.

⁵ For an elaboration of this process of growth, see James M. Reese, "Patterns of Ministry in the New Testament as Interpreting the Role of the Permanent Diaconate," *American Ecclesiastical Review* 166 (March 1972) 174–184.

⁶ Robert W. Funk addresses the problem of "clearing away the obfuscating debris" hindering the saving hearing of the biblical text in his article "Beyond Criticism in Quest of Literacy: The Parable of the Leaven," *Interpretation* 25 (April 1971) 149–170.

⁷See note 1 of chapter 1.

NOTES TO CHAPTER FIVE, pages 60–79

¹ For reflections about the importance of "memorizing" or envisioning the entire composition as a whole, see J. Gauvin, "Interprétation et lexicographie dans le domaine de la philosophie," *Recherches de Science Religieuse* 61 (1973) 119–126.

² Charles H. Giblin, *In Hope of God's Glory* (New York: Herder and Herder, 1970) calls attention to this need for an adequate appreciation of Paul's letters. An example of his approach is found in "A Reading of Paul's Gospel: Romans 1–8," *The Bible Today* 60 (April, 1972) 753–761.

³ Better understanding of primitive Christianity is forcing what James M. Robinson calls the dismantling and reassembling of categories of New Testament scholarship in the first chapter of the series of studies he published jointly with H. Koester, *Trajectories through Early Christianity* (Philadelphia: Fortress, 1971).

⁴ X. Léon-Dufour sees this growth as expressing Paul's experience of the risen Lord Jesus, in chapter 3 of his penetrating study, *Résurrection de Jésus et message pascal* (Paris: Seuil, second edition 1972).

⁵ Pope Paul VI discussed this responsibility in his talk to the XXI Italian Biblical Week, referred to above in chapter 1.

⁶ For a manifesto of a biblical scholar proposing "a mode of Bible study which facilitates transformation in human lives," see Walter Wink, *The Bible in Human Transformation: Toward a New Paradigm for Biblical Study* (Philadelphia: Fortress Press, 1973).

⁷ The term was popularized in a collection of essays by J. M. Robinson and H. Koester mentioned in note 3; it now appears frequently in biblical writings.

⁸ J. Dupont discusses this enfleshing of oral preaching in the introduction to his study of the beatitudes, published in the Etudes Bibliques series, *Les Béatitudes 1: Le problème littéraire* (Paris: J. Gabalda, 1969), 9–40.

⁹ Eugene A. Nida, "Implications of Contemporary Linguistics for Biblical Scholarship," *Journal of Biblical Literature* 91 (March, 1972) 73–89, 81.

¹⁰ See Norman Perrin, "Towards an Interpretation of the Gospel of Mark,"

in H. D. Betz, ed., *Christology and a Modern Pilgrimage* (Claremont: New Testament Colloquium, 1971) 1–78.

[11] J. Louis Martyn, *History and Theology in the Gospel of John* (New York: Harper and Row, 1968).

[12] See John H. Elliott, "Ministry and Church Order in the New Testament: A Traditio-Historical Analysis (1 Peter 5:1-5)", *Catholic Biblical Quarterly* 32 (July, 1970), 367–391.

NOTES TO CHAPTER SIX, pages 80–93

[1] See Louis Dupré, *The Other Dimension: A Search for the Meaning of Religious Attitudes* (Garden City: Doubleday & Co., 1972) 296–297.

[2] See Walter B. Wink's comments in a review of a technical study by W. G. Thompson in *Catholic Biblical Quarterly* 34 (1972) 123–124. Also his book *The Bible in Human Transformation: Toward a New Paradigm for Biblical Studies* (Philadelphia: Fortress Press, 1974) with review in *Catholic Biblical Quarterly* 36 (1974) 295–296.

[3] E. Schweizer, *Jesus* (Richmond: John Knox, 1971), 16. See also C. H. Dodd, *The Founder of Christianity* (New York: Macmillan, 1970).

[4] This is pretty much what W. Marxsen said in the famous talk he gave in 1964 on "The Resurrection of Jesus as a Historical and Theological Problem," in C. F. Moule, ed., *The Significance of the Message of the Resurrection for Faith in Jesus Christ* (Naperville: Allenson, 1968).

[5] Comment made by Raymond Brown in the 1970 Brussels' World Congress on the future of the Church.

[6] See above in chapter 2, note 8.

[7] On the role of these discourses as explaining how Jesus remains, see James M. Reese, "Literary Structure of John 13:31–14:31; 16:5–6, 16–33," *Catholic Biblical Quarterly* 34 (1972) 321–331.

[8] See Edward P. Echlin, S. J., "Crisis in Preaching" *Commonweal* 94 (August 20, 1971) 423–426.

NOTES TO CHAPTER SEVEN, pages 94–106

[1] For example, A. M. Hunter, "The Interpreter and the Parables," in R. Batey, ed., *New Testament Issues* (New York: Harper and Row, 1970) 71–87, counts some 55 parables and estimates that they occupy about 35% of the Lord's teachings in the gospels.

[2] See *The Gospel According to Thomas* (New York: Harper & Brothers, 1959) for an early Coptic sayings-collection that contains interesting variations on the parables of the canonical gospels. Since the parables in the Gospel of Thomas contain at times elements more primitive than details in the Synoptic Gospels, the evangelists adapted the parables of Jesus to the needs of their audience.

[3] C. H. Dodd, *The Parables of the Kingdom* (New York: Charles Scribner's Sons; revised edition, 1961). The original edition dates from 1935.

[4] J. Jeremias, *The Parables of Jesus* (New York: Charles Scribner's Sons, 1965). This is translated from the sixth German edition.

[5] R. W. Funk, *Language, Hermeneutic and Word of God* (New York: Harper and Row, 1966) 244.

[6] J. D. Crossan, "The Seed Parables of Jesus," *Journal of Biblical Literature* 92 (1973) 244–266; 266.

[7] *Ibid.*, 265. He calls them "ontologico-poetic articulation."

[8] Amos N. Wilder, *Early Christian Rhetoric: The Language of the Gospels* (Cambridge: Harvard University Press, 1971) 71.

[9] J. D. Crossan, "Parable and Example in the Teaching of Jesus," *New Testament Studies* 18 (1971–72) 285–307; 304–305.

[10] R. W. Funk, *Language*, (see note 5) 236.

[11] Compare H. Urs von Balthasar's esthetical theology as outlined in *Love Alone* (New York: Herder and Herder, 1969).

[12] R. W. Funk, "The Parables: A Fragmentary Agenda," in D. G. Miller, ed., *Jesus and Man's Hope* (Pittsburgh: Pittsburgh Theological Seminary, 1971) vol. 2, 287–303.

[13] Pope Paul VI in his address to the XXI Italian Biblical Week (see chapter 1, note 1).

[14] R. W. Funk, *Language* (see note 5) 16–17.

[15] R. W. Funk, "Beyond Criticism in Quest of Literacy: the Parable of the Leaven," *Interpretation* 25 (1971) 149–170; 164.

[16] J. D. Crossan, "Parable and Example," (see note 9) 301.

[17] See Dan O. Via, Jr., "The Relationship of Form to Content in the Parables: The Wedding Feast," *Interpretation* 25 (1971) 171–184.

NOTES TO CHAPTER EIGHT, pages 107–128

[1] Karl Rahner, "Theos in the New Testament," *Theological Investigations* (London: Darton, Longman and Todd, 1961) I. 79–148.

[1a] It should be noted that this expression appears in Gal. 2:16,20;3:22,26; Rom. 3:22,26; Phil. 3:9 although English versions usually render it "faith in Christ," obscuring the paradox to some extent.

[2] C. Spicq, in his lectures on Love in the New Testament at the University of Fribourg, Switzerland, 1956–1957. See also his *Théologie morale du Nouveau Testament*, 2 vol. (Paris: J. Gabalda, 1965).

[3] National Conference of Catholic Bishops, *The Program of Priestly Formation* (Washington, D.C., 1971) #4.

[4] Given at the Salesian Institute sponsored by the Order of the Vistation in Vienna, Virginia, August 1970.

[5] Karl Rahner, "The Dignity and Freedom of Man," *Theological Investigations I* (London: Darton, Longman and Todd, 1963) 235–263, especially 238, 246–247.

[6] Karl Rahner, "Remark on the Dogmatic Treatise 'De Trinitate,'" *Theological Investigations IV* (London: Darton, Longman and Todd, 1966) 77–102.

[7] James Chereso, "Religious Experience and Atheism" in G. Devine, ed., *New Dimensions in Religious Experience* (New York: Alba House, 1971) 155–172.

[8] See Dewart, *The Future of Belief* (New York: Herder and Herder, 1966) 147–148.

General Bibliography

L. Alonso Shökel, *The Inspired Word*. New York: Herder and Herder, 1965.

John L. Austin, *How to Do Things with Words*. New York: Oxford University Press, 1965.

R. Barthes and others, *Structural Analysis and Biblical Exegesis*. Pittsburgh: The Pickwick Press, 1974.

William A. Beardslee, *Literary Criticism of the New Testament*. Philadelphia: Fortress Press, 1970.

Frederick W. Danker, *Jesus and the New Age According to St. Luke: A Commentary on the Third Gospel*. St. Louis: Clayton Publishing House, 1972.

Charles H. Dodd, *The Founder of Christianity*. New York: Macmillan, 1970.

William G. Doty, *Contemporary New Testament Interpretation*. Englewood Cliffs, N.J.: Prentice-Hall, 1972.

Robert W. Funk, *Language, Hermeneutic, and Word of God*. New York: Harper and Row, 1966.

Jerry G. Gill, *The Possibility of Religious Knowledge*. Grand Rapids: Eerdmans, 1971.

Wilfrid J. Harrington, *Parables Told by Jesus*. New York: Alba House, 1974.

Stanley Romaine Hopper and David L. Miller, eds., *Interpretation: The Poetry of Meaning*. New York: Harcourt, Brace and World, 1967.

Joachim Jeremias, *The Parables of Jesus*. 6th ed, New York: Charles Scribner's Sons, 1963.

Robert J. Karris, *Following Jesus: A Guide to the Gospels*. Chicago: Franciscan Herald Press, 1973.

Jack D. Kingsbury, *The Parables of Jesus in Matthew 13*. Richmond: J. Knox Press, 1969.

Xavier Léon-Dufour, *Resurrection and the Message of Easter*. New York: Holt, Rinehart, and Winston, 1975.

John Lyons, *Introduction to Theoretical Linguistics*. New York: Cambridge U. Press, 1968.

J. L. Martyn, *History and Theology in the Fourth Gospel*. New York: Harper and Row, 1968.

Eugene A. Nida, *Religion across Cultures: A Study in the Communication of Christian Faith*. New York: Harper & Row, 1968.

Eugene A. Nida and C. R. Taber, *The Theory and Practice of Translation*. Leiden: E. J. Brill, 1969.

134

Gerald O'Collins, *The Resurrection of Jesus Christ.* Valley Forge, Pa.: Judson Press, 1973.

Norman Perrin, *The New Testament, an Introduction.* New York: Harcourt, Brace, Jovanovich, 1974.

Paul Ricoeur, *The Conflict of Interpretation: Essays in Hermeneutics.* Evanston: Northwestern U. Press, 1974.

James M. Robinson and John B. Cobb, Jr., eds., *The New Hermeneutic.* New York: Harper and Row, 1964.

Donald Senior, *Matthew: A Gospel for the Church.* Chicago: Franciscan Herald Press, 1973.

Thomas J. Smith, *The Mighty Message of Mark.* Winona, Minn: St. Mary's College Press, 1973.

G. N. Stanton, *Jesus of Nazareth in New Testament Preaching.* N.Y.: Cambridge U. Press, 1973.

S. M. TeSelle, *Speaking in Parables.* Philadelphia: Fortress Press, 1975.

Paul Van Buren, *The Edges of Language: An Essay in the Logic of Religion.* London: S.C.M. Press, 1972.

Dan O. Via, Jr., *The Parables.* Philadelphia: Fortress, 1967.

R. Welleck & A. Warren, *A Theory of Literature.* New York: Harcourt, Brace and World, 1956.

Amos M. Wilder, *The New Voice.* New York: Herder and Herder, 1969.

————*Early Christian Rhetoric: The Language of the Gospel.* Cambridge: Harvard University Press, 1971; reissue with new introduction.